KIRKE WISE
VOL. 1 FUN WITH WORDS

POEMS TO THE PEOPLE

NOT JUST ANOTHER POETRY BOOK
WARNING: CONTAINS RHYMES

KIRKE WISE
VOL. 1 FUN WITH WORDS

POEMS TO
THE PEOPLE

NOT JUST ANOTHER POETRY BOOK
WARNING: CONTAINS RHYMES

FOREWORD
Kelly A. Mechling

Kirke Wise is a wise old owl.

No, not an owl, exactly; but he *is* wise, and his poems do take flight.

A spirited writer with a poetic consciousness and an exacting craftmanship, Kirke is a word spinner. His poems dance, dazzle, delight. They scintillate, surprise, sparkle, or soothe, depending on the mood.

Sometimes his words flash like colored pulsing LED lights, hypnotizing the reader into ecstatic rhythm. Other times his words become swords, fighting darkness and evil, falseness and foibles.

Most of the time, though, his words are gracious, heartwarming, whimsical, playful, and relatable. There's a homespun quality to his verses that offers a sense of comfort and familiarity, reminiscent of those by early twentieth-century poet Edgar Guest, known as the "People's Poet." Both poets write from a place of groundedness, common sense, humor, optimism, and nostalgia.

Kirke's poems, however, aren't all about looking back at the past at "what was." They often launch us into the future, into the unknown, into the mind-bending realm of "what if." A poet of keen perception, curiosity, and vision, Kirke's mind is nimble and as busy as a pinball machine; the cognitive wheels are constantly spinning, imagining, inventing. He thinks like an engineer, an engineer of creation.

Reading Kirke's poems is like joyriding through space and time: he transports us to far-off galaxies, traveling deep into the mysteries of the universe, or he steers us back into our hearts while visiting the places and people we loved from our past. Over and over again we are drawn to his verses, those new or nostalgic spaces where we can explore, linger, savor, feel.

Kirke's passion for writing and self-expression brings to mind one of my favorite quotes by James Michener: "I love writing. I love the swirl and swing of words as they tangle with human emotions." Swirl, swing, tangle....! Jazzy! This is Kirke's mind, on words.

Kirke is both Renaissance Man and Salt of the Earth. A man with eclectic interests and a multitude of projects (hügelkultur, raising chickens, sustainable composting, solar panels, electronic systems, building and repurposing computers, radio broadcasting, with winemaking being the latest), Kirke is an expert in using tools, and his creative ingenuity is unmatched. (As one of Kirke's friends likes to say, Kirke is the only person he knows who can go into a junkyard with a roll of duct tape and come out with a yacht.) Words are *also* his tools; every poem he builds is a bridge to his readers.

Kirke does not write from the Ivory Tower. No highbrow elitist poems here. His are Poems for the People. Accessible, relatable, inspirational, profound. They are not meant to garner accolades or applause, but rather to touch people's hearts, to lift people's spirits, to offer comfort and encouragement, to jar the imagination, to guide us to new places in the mind. These poetic journeys, whether deep into space or deep into our hearts, are driven by Kirke's passion for language, for communication, for creative exploration. Connecting with people through verse is his ultimate mission.

During the past five years, Kirke has written over one thousand poems. Seven hundred have been posted on social media; seventeen have been published in *The Watershed Journal*. To describe him as "prolific" would be an understatement. His passion for writing and sharing his verses is commendable.

Kirke once said that his writing is "unashamed and unrestrained." I have always found his writing to be honest, humble, and thought-provoking. His poems celebrate what it means to be human. His poems have a pulse. A heartbeat. Whether about long-passed parents or unrequited love, Kirke's poems enrich us, enlighten us, make us better people.

Every poem by Kirke Wise is a gift to his readers.

Please accept Kirke's latest gift – a treasure trove of his collected poems – and allow yourself to be lifted: three, two, one . . . *blast-off*! As you rise up into his new poetic frontier, let Kirke's words shine like stars and illuminate your soul.

Kelly A. Mechling is a Ph.D. in English. Originally from Clarion, Pennsylvania, and a long-time friend of Kirke Wise, she teaches Literature, Memoir, and Creative Writing at a private college in New England.

PREFACE
Kirke Wise

If I were ever to go into a large room filled with everyday people and enthusiastically proclaim: "I just wrote a new poetry book!" I know exactly what would happen.

First, there would be a certain small number of people who would carefully make their way towards the exit in an orderly fashion, much like the proverbial "yelling fire in a theater" scenario. Of course, there might be a few who would panic and run out as well. But they would all simply be trying to avoid the future pain, in this case, being under the expected subjugation of the coming delivery of a long, boring, and bland intellectual pontification of sorts. This is stereotypical of what most everyday folk might think modern poetry is comprised of today. I know many people who see it exactly that way as well. They're simply not interested. I can certainly understand that view, considering the present world we live in. We no longer live the simple lives of yesteryear, where entertainment was essentially only through books, plays, and gatherings.

We're busy with our lives and have an unlimited amount of easy-to-digest information and entertainment at our fingertips. So many different sorts of specific areas to beinterested in as well. Things that simply didn't exist in the past. Like almost everything, in fact, that we have in the world today…

There are many people, however, who still love plain old literature and poetry. I think that's a wonderful thing! It ranges from simply being an avid reader to also writing, with some even further appreciating the exact usage of words and the many technicalities of perfect composition.

And that's an art form and science that I respect. These would be among the relatively small number of people in that room that might say, "that's neat, a new poetry book." I don't think there would be very many, though. The rest of us have other interests to pursue, after all. I myself have a myriad of other fields and interests that I hold far closer to and identify with. Other forms of entertainment as well. So, I'm like those other countless people in that respect. The unwashed masses, if you will. But we do all like to have fun.

How could poetry of any type ever effectively compete in today's modern world of distractions? Perhaps by making them fun and easy to understand?

In my case, I'm a hands-on sort of person. I like to dream up all kinds of crazy ideas and put them into action, like using electronics and miniature home-built computer controls to make my life easier. Perhaps monitor my house, scare deer from my garden, or lock my chickens in their coop at night, etc. I have many other interests and hobbies also. But I'm always very technically minded, and I tend to want to create anything I make in an organized and efficient way. Both cost-effective and bulletproof in its reliability. Designed for worst-case operation so that it never ever fails. Because I think like an inventor and an engineer, that's me. And most of all, whatever I do must be enjoyable and fun. Life's hard enough without having to further labor away in your "free time."

And that's precisely the subconsciously driven methodology that my poems were based upon since day one. Simplicity, ease of use, functionality, efficiency, cost-effectiveness (in this case, time), and appeal. But also to be of an intuitive design. Like a complex machine that is also very easy to handle and run. One that was designed to be organic and natural. And certainly, one which doesn't require any training or classroom instruction to be able to fully comprehend and utilize. A device for all both great and small.

Although I'm a builder at heart, I found myself starting to write trite little poems one day. It wasn't something that I would have ever thought I'd be doing either! But I did. And it was fun in a way. Almost like a mental challenge of sorts. Something I've often likened to solving a crossword puzzle that you're also writing. But I'm not so much interested in those sorts of challenges either. I've always had countless other things to keep my mind busy.

With a little bit of time, things started to change. It became easier to write poems and much more fun, too. I didn't worry or fret about making them in just a certain way. I just wrote them out. I was doing it for fun anyway, so it wasn't a big deal. In fact, it got to the point where something inside of me would prompt me to write one even if I didn't really feel like it. I genuinely believe the poems came from the depths of my mind. A mind that really enjoyed it and just wanted to have fun. I've explained this before as being like a kid at home and having some other kids come over knocking on the door wanting me to go out to play. In this case, my mind wanted me to write more poems.

And now, many of them almost write themselves from out of my inner being and creativity. Usually with the title first, and then line upon line and stanza after stanza until it's finished. The slightest thing can spark one of these. A word, the rhythm of a song, something I say, a feeling, the look on another's face, etc. I don't often refuse those impromptu prompts anymore, either. Because when I do, the words fade away as quickly as they came to me. And none of this is only on an intellectual level. That's not so much what I do. I simply write what's inside of me. From my memories, my emotions, my creativity, and my imagination. Some things I've personally experienced as well as many more that have come from other people's lives.

Some of these poems are strange and fanciful; others are simply comedic in nature. But there are many more that are dead serious. About our feelings across life, our hopeful desires or regrets. About what we might find within our own selves if we choose to look. And it's all very genuine if you can accept it for what it is. These have been written from the heart of the young man who still lives inside me as well as the little kid there who likes to have fun. The person who's been scared of an uncertain future before as well as the person who always has such great hope. Also, from me in the present, as I navigate through this 21 st century with the rest of you. But what they all have in common is that they're all down to earth in an open and very unguarded way.

That's the same way I also live my own present life. I've always been very unashamed and unrestrained in what I've written. There's no reason that any of us really needs to hide. Hiding behind our hedges of pride or self-delusion or in any basements of disappointment or bitterness. We're all just simple humans inside. We face the very same obstacles. Either to surmount them or to succumb to them. I want everyone to rise above all of that to become better and more content people.

You'll never see any of the light at all when you're hiding, as we're all so prone to do.

So, I'd like you to approach this book with an open heart and an open mind, considering that's exactly how I wrote it. Not to critically read it as if it's something to be looked upon and evaluated, but rather to allow yourself to feel it. Because many of these poems were written solely from raw emotion and creativity. Those many raw materials being the very components that my poems were built from.

Many people have been able to see them in this way over the several years that I've posted them on social media. I've been fortunate to have had an overwhelmingly positive response to the poems I've put out there. I heard many times from people who said that it was precisely what they needed to see that day in that particular time of their lives. Or that they felt as if the poem was about them or even directed to them. To illuminate their feelings or perhaps codify their innermost secret thoughts and fears. And I think that's the most that any poet could ever hope for their work to achieve. So be open to these poems and let them in. If any of them ring a bell inside you, consider it yours. Written to you, about you, beside you, despite you, from you, and by you. Your poem, in other words. If my poems serve to help anyone in any way, then I've done my job.

But I have a job for you as well. Make sure you let go occasionally. Let your own inner kid come out from behind the hedges and up from the basements. Let yourself dream and imagine. Feel the warmth of the bright sunshine. Not just the sun above, but the one in you.

Jump off your cliff of fears. You won't fall. You'll fly.

TABLE OF CONTENTS

Are you ready to turn modern poetry "on its head"?

(Photo by: Jodie Beabout)

PART ONE:
fun with words

Quality Tea

It couldn't transport me,
That mug that I bought.
Full of some tepid tea,
Or at least so I thought.

It was way off the norm
And exceedingly hot!
Far above the lukewarm
Like a thermal onslaught!

When I like to buy myself some tea,
I want it just right and only for me,
Calming my mouth so my palette runs free
For some quality tea, that's the key!

And as that hot tea will certainly burn,
The baristas fumbled as they took their turn,
Being full of confusion and self-concern
My only question is? Will they ever learn…

For I went to the shop as a last resort,
Only wanting a drink for caffeine transport.
Take my mind away and above the clouds,
But now I'm spitting out tea as I gasp out loud!

But I'm no wanna-be coffee shop amateur.
I'm a slow-sipping caffeine connoisseur
With no time for any teacup saboteur!
So, I left in great haste as I called my chauffeur!

Facebook Birthday

Facebook birthdays are always the best
For the comments, posts, or even a "like."
Putting your "friends" list to the ultimate test,
And if they don't post,
                    they can all take a hike!

It's a time for them to wish you well,
A way to spread some digital cheer.
And if they don't,
          they can go straight to hell!
Because the "unfriend" button is always near...

You won't get money or cakes and stuff,
But it's good when they can wish you well.
Those internet greetings are more than enough
As those simple gestures have so much to tell.

In a town with so many virtual connections
Being rather apart, yet all still here,
A way of transcending our imperfections
And those good intentions will never disappear.

16

Tire Shop

I found myself sitting at the tire shop,
Awaiting my time in a very long line.
Hearing the hubcaps and lug nuts drop,
Hoping my tire change turned out fine.

Pondering about the coming weather—
Being icy and cold or muddy and slick—
Silently sitting and wondering whether
Those tires would slide or loyally stick.

Air tools wailed as they torqued and tightened,
A balancing act of the wheels for sure.
Though I'm not a driver who's easily frightened,
I needed good treads for my daily grand tour.

Because I'm a traveler of many miles,
Traversing the roads and hills all around
To meet the challenge of my roadway trials,
I need the best tires that can ever be found.

Black Friday

'Twas the month before Christmas
And all through the store,
The shoppers were swarming
As they all blocked the door.

Moving frantically
As they made their way
Though stuffed with turkey
From the previous day.

Looking for deals,
A bargain, a steal
To add stuff to their life
As if that were real.

Searching for goods
At a much lower cost
While being so careful
Their kids didn't get lost.

Then next year will come
And your old things will go,
Making space in your place
For the next year's show.

Tip the Baristas

Don't forget to tip the baristas,
And don't be overly mean!
Lest they then overly sugar
Or skimp on your coveted cream!

Give them all your money!
Or maybe a little change will do.
You would come to see the light
If that poor barista was you!

And clean up all your dishes!
While policing your grungy cups
Then wiping up your spills,
They'll appreciate it all so much!

And always be ever thankful
For that place you always drink,
Sipping your very own coffee
With some quality time to think...

Trick or Treat

It's not what it seems, that Halloween
As the ghosts and the goblins fill the air
With the ominous air of evil intent.
Children proceed without any care.

It's just pretty neat
That trick or treat,
With a bag full of candy
That can't be beat.

With the careful guidance of their parent's care,
Though the costumed monsters will surely abound,
It's certainly a time that they're willing to dare
With plenty of booty from the houses around.

And all through the night, enduring their fright,
There's a certain feeling of serenity
Because that night will end, where they had to defend
Then back to their own comfortable family.

Roller Derby Queen

The Roller Derby Queen
On her royal wheels
Comes into the scene
Amid howls and squeals.

Take that with a smash!
As the divas clash
With moves bold and brash,
As they "take out the trash."

We're gonna bust some teeth,
You little bitches!
Give you some grief,
Put you in stitches!

The only fair play was a turnabout,
As blockers spit "hockers" during the bout.
Gotta be quick, with no time to think,
Fighting for your life in the roller rink.

With a mash and a crash, mostly for show
While skating in circles, resisting their foe,
But even though they were strong and lean,
They were actually nice and not that mean.

All working together to win it their way
As a Roller Derby Queen after so much play.

Roller Station

She roller-skated through the corridors,
Her steel wheels on the magnetic floor.
There was something unique in her persona
That I simply couldn't help but adore.

The visiting dignitary called it an aberration!
I heard the captain tell him, "Not so fast.
She's the best of our space station's commanders."
As with a determined purpose, she skated past....

"She can't be burdened by the clunk of a magnetic boot."
"And too valuable to be working outside in a spacesuit."
"She runs things as only a woman like her could do."
"If I want to stay in command, I may need to skate too!"

Being only a cadet meant this didn't pertain to me,
But the purity of her purpose was so beautiful to see.
Attending so many duties by her singular magnetic spin,
Far better than an old space boot's clumsily clunking din.

I just wondered... if I could somehow learn to skate.
Maybe, just maybe, I might get a date...

The Simple Things

It's the "every day" of our lives,
Those little things that bring us joy,
Or the times we feel perplexed,
Those moments we felt destroyed.

With our walks by the waters,
Countless streams that carry us along.
There are so many reflections to remember
As we've struggled to sing a better song...

To find contentment against the eddies,
Trying for stability within those waves,
Skirting the very edges of eternity,
With the optimism that so often saves.

With each experience and challenge
Regardless of the outcome it brings,
Just simply trying until we're almost crying,
Holding on to those hopes of the simple things...

Autumn Leaves

When the first autumn leaves
Start to gently come down,
They signal the change
That comes to our town.

All the orange and yellow
Only add to that flair,
Looking forward to fun
With goodwill in the air.

Because every year
In that special time,
The colors of our trees
Are in their own prime.

The Autumn Leaf Festival
In Clarion, P. A.
When we all come together
With those leaves on display.

fun with words

Moments we'll never forget

"poems to the people gives power to the
people"

"fishing for rhymes within the depths
of our minds"

Such a Thing!

The flowers come out
And the birds start to sing
As the bees are buzzing
For a hopeful new spring.

The animals will play
On those sunny days
From the warmth of wisdom
In nature's own ways.

The oppressive coldness
Of a dark winter's mind,
And we're all so willing
To leave it all behind…

I'm so very thankful
That there is such a thing!
Towards a new beginning
With the advent of spring.

Clearly Dirty

"Don't move the rocks!"
As she said long ago,
Ages before machines,
Our ancient Sappho.

She didn't know about me
Or our diesel power,
The progress of man,
Our industrial flower.

And unlike "Spappho",
I'm digging as I please,
Splitting through the grit,
Excavating with ease.

For I have a Kubota
And I'm skilled with its stick.
I dig where I want to;
It's really pretty slick.

And I'll dig as I may,
I shall dig as I might,
Grinding gears by the day
And unearthing by the night.

I'm a child of evolution,
An industrial revolution,
Backhoes do as I say,
Hydraulics lead the way.

And I've taken over
With rocks at my command
To dig all that I please
That Sappho be damned.

Those Daffodils
After Willian Wordsworth

I just couldn't contain myself
In the simple wonderment before my eyes
By such a serene scene of serendipity
As if it had all been touched...
From the very heart of those sun-filled skies.

In the deepest times that we'd hoped to remember
Because the sunshine was never in vain,
Slowly warming our ultimate surrender
When we would never again be the same...

Because across the brook
And around so many trees,
Nature would make a way for them
So the flowers could do as they please.

In glowing shows of effervescence,
A natural beauty we could easily see,
The very lives of those simple flowers,
The trying times meant to set us free...

For a lifetime past the plain and simple,
A chance to exist and never again resist...
To seed the landscape with all your might
As the dreams of those flowers always persist.

To cover the cares of our earthbound troubles,
Those fields of daffodils are a beautiful sight...

"Grammer-nazie"

If I were a grammar Nazi,
                I'd correct every single post!

Showing all of the world
   who really knows the most!

Jumping into those grammatical frays
So I could teach a more enlightened way.

But I write without rules only using my wits,
Throwing literary Illuminati into great fits!

I'm a talker, not a "typer"; what more can I do
But my poorly-written poems will still ring true.

Eventually, I'll have some more Grammarly ways
And my verse will be perfected in those future days.

But for the time being, I can just barely spell,
Keeping the "Literazis" in their un-writing hell!

And when I'm long passed and my pen is retired,
The many people who read me will be re-inspired.

But future Grammar Nazis will say, "What the hell?
This guy broke the rules! And he can barely spell!!!!"

Happy Birthday, Dr. Suess!

His name was Dr. Seuss,
And he really loved to rhyme.
He never needed an excuse,
So he rhymed most all of the time

And he even had a cat,
A cartoonish aristocrat!
It was a cat that wore a hat!
Now, what do you think about that!

In the distant, magical land of Katroo.
There's a birthday party and a great ballyhoo,
And Horton is hearing all of The Who's
As they all sing happy birthday to you!

Although the Grinch stole Christmas,
He still got you a special gift
For your famous birthday party
Because you're so dearly missed.

A fox in socks will be there too,
Along with little Cindy-Lou Who.
Of course, with Thing One as well as Thing Two,
And that old Once-ler and the rest of the crew.

And Sally will also be coming
Along with Sam-I-Am,
And surely that guy-am-I
Is gonna bring the green eggs and ham!

The Lorax and Little Cat Z
Are gonna be right there with me
With a Wocket in my extra pocket
Beside all the Truffula trees.

And Bartholomew Cubbins
With the many various Sneetches,
And those brown Bar-ba-loots
With the other Nizzards and creatures… Happy Birthday!

If I Could Write

If I could relate
Some simple truths about life,
To separate the darkness
And illuminate it with lights...

If I could imagine
A much higher human plane,
Maybe I'd try to get there
And things would never be quite the same...

If I could remember
The various trials of our race,
Miles upon endless miles
I could throw it back in your face...

If I could write,
Perhaps no one would listen
About our cares in this world
And our angst about the forbidden...

If I were emboldened
To take that very step,
Giving it all or nothing
In the truth of my promises kept...

If I could imagine
A far greater place,
I'd lay a foundation of purity
And I'd be writing from outer space...

About the pains and the gains
Or the forces of remorse,
The quiet within every riot
Our marriages and divorce.

But I'm not any kind of writer.
I just build things every day,
Technological innovations
With just a little bit left over to say...
            I'm getting there...

Poetic Prevention

Crisis intervention,
Poetic prevention,
You can only say
What we think's okay!

Creative constraints,
Artistic detention,
We're the snobs who rule
Lest we failed to mention!

God forbid
Better seal the lid
And shut your door
So you'll write no more!

How dare you try
To make readers cry
By your rhyming curse
In unmetered verse!

We've destroyed it,
And we're in control
Why so many hate it
For losing its soul!

It can't entertain,
Certainly, no fun
By rules ingrained,
Creations undone!

From ivory towers,
We'll judge it all,
As poetry flounders,
Continuing its fall!

And it's okay
While we have our say
With writing unread
Because it's so dead!

Finished?

Is a poem really ever finished?
With the things, it has to say,
Constantly being refinished
While it slowly makes its way?

Is a line really ever perfected?
As a mirror for the very soul,
Or is that picture somehow rejected
With the verse falling short of its goal?

Is a poet then somehow diminished?
Trying to express our innermost strife,
Never leaving any thoughts unfinished
For unlocking the very keys of life?

Has the writer then somehow neglected?
To breathe life from their innermost style
Or just waiting for the ones preselected
To heal some hearts every once in a while?

Drive-by Poet

I've always been a little bit of a gangster
In my old Australian Bush hat.
Although I was so much younger,
I've never fully escaped all of that.

Always so controversial
And forever pushing the norm
Because of my imaginary explosions
That was just part of my everyday form.

So, I guess I haven't changed that much,
Being enamored by the mind's pretty lights,
The imaginations of what could be there
As well as getting into my own share of fights.

As the stoic tough guy that I used to be,
Brazen beyond any need to reform,
Valuing liberty and my need to remain free
In balance between the paranormal and the norm.

But at least I had a good vocabulary....
Many things I shouldn't even say to this day,
The machinations of an evil genius unhinged,
My imagination always demanding to play.

Although my parents and teachers always cringed...

That's why it seems to come so easy for me,
Although at first it was certainly not.
It's from the many battles of my life's story
To love understanding those battles I fought.

Rat a tat tat! ... ...
Now what do you think about that?
A drive-by poet's machine gun... ...
It's where our inner mind is truly at.

It's much easier to use a submachine gun,
But that would spill blood all over the place.
And you know what? This poetry is a lot of fun;
I get a chance to place some wisdom in your face.

Never scared of any open mic
Regardless of what the audience is like,
And if they don't seem to get it
Well, they can all just take a hike...

Because I'm not that scared of anyone.
I'm ready for the zombie apocalypse!
It's the very essence of my inner being
Because only a dead man perpetually sits...

All the fancy words I might carefully conjure—
Well, I simply couldn't give a damn.
Simplicity is the very key to the future,
And I do it for the simple reason that I can...

So, I traded my AK-47
For a few straight words that are so much fun
Into a completely different fortune
No longer having to be on the run.

Bang bang bang! ...
I shot you in the head! ...
If you can only grasp the simplicity
Of what I've written to be transparently read...

Then I'll kick some ass
And then take some names...
And don't you just know it...
I grew up to become a drive-by poet...

Give it Up

I was wandering through my sunlit gardens,
The stuff of life when it begins to turn ripe.
But there was a trip that was waiting for me
Like an *Alice in Wonderland* archetype...

With just a little inconspicuous rabbit,
So far below our understanding of life,
One of those simple little creatures of habit,
Never being embroiled in our human strife.

But he stopped his routine to look up at me
As if some communication had come into play.
The many freedoms that we rarely realize
There were a few things he wanted to say to me.

"Whoa! You've got to give it up–
The unwillingness to leave your nonsensical style!
You must see past the dreams of human motivations;
It's so fulfilling to experience reality once in a while.

"The pains against the gains, as you go insane,
Immediacies of such a short-lived compensation
As if any of you were ever really to blame...
While fighting against your own life's continuation...

"Because the truths that seem to be so very simple
Will be the things that will always continue to live,
But the self-centricity of your own lives of servitude
Will strip away anything that you could ever hope to give.

"But whoa! You better give it all up,
And you'd better start on a new path right now.
I know I'm just a simple rabbit, an animal of habit,
But you people better get your act together, holy cow!"

And I took this advice a little bit unwillingly,
Just at first, because of the thirst for my superiority,
But perhaps these simple creatures and their principals
Could lead us all to a more fulfilling harmony...

Battlespace

We're going to rev our bikes
And load up our guns,
Gonna change some rules
So poems can be fun.

Activate our missiles
Blasting through the sky,
Controlling the airspace
Before poetry dies.

We'll hit them with our chains
Rumbling in the streets.
We're the new gang in town,
Crashing the poetry meets.

Riding on steel tanks,
Crushing the land of BLAH,
By imagination's ranks
With things you never saw.

Because we're real men,
And we know what's right.
We ride in pickup trucks,
Knowing how to fight.

And we will float above,
Attacking from outer space
The world's literal oysters
We can see from that place.

And we're also grounded,
Coming up from below.
You shall be confounded
By what we really know.

Listening to discourse far and wide,
Carefully weighing what was said.
No longer wanting to run and hide,
Cutting through the crap of what is read.

And don't you think you'll get away
As we rewrite it all and save the day,
Because we can see what this world needs,
Knowing what the future readers will read.

36

Buckling beauty

How do we not stop and buckle?
With the sheer beauty of it all,
Through warm summer rains
Then the painted leaves of fall.

Mountains spanning coastlines
All covered in a mysterious mist,
The complexity of creation
Creating this endless list.

Atomic stars full of power
That beam across the voids of space
To a planet of life and emotion
With a still and particular grace.

Countless fields full of flowers
With their colors all astray,
The singular sunrise and sunset
Declaring each bright new day.

Animals of every kind found
Living in their own special place,
Diverse expressions of complexity
With a sculpture upon each face.

Countless butterflies flitting,
The birds of the skies all soar.
The scope of this symphony
Is something you can't ignore.

Colorful Trees

The thing about those autumn leaves
Is that they come from the most colorful trees,
All gently falling to the ground
As fall's cool winds wisp around.

Slowly swaying by nature's ways,
Painting the pictures that nature says,
Preparing the way for their winter's sleep,
Showing a brightness your thoughts can keep.

Living in silence while saying much more,
The artists of the forest that we adore,
Making the animals a winter home;
These are the trees that we've all known.

Surrounding pastures and covering hills
With forested blankets as nature wills,
Growing tall and seeking the light,
Those graceful trees before our sight.

April Mud

April showers were bringing May's flowers,
Raining for hours from the higher powers.
Too much is wet and turning to mud,
Starting to fret with my shoes full of crud.

Under duress from this muddy mess,
A way to depress as we must all confess,
In waterproof suits with our muddy boots,
Making substitutes to take the drier routes.

Is there any way to have a warm spring day?
Or too much to pray that it isn't so gray?
To be sunny and mild just like a song–
We have waited and waited way too long!

We all said goodbye to winter's way,
Hoping the warmth would be here to stay.
A springtime meadow we were looking to find,
Now finding ourselves in this muddy bind.

But there's lots of rain for a very good reason—
We will forget our pain in the coming season.
Fields of flowers for the warm summer days,
From the April showers of nature's ways.

Coming Home

In a tall, dark forest, among the ferns,
No stars would stay to show me the way,
But by peaceful paths through twists and turns,
The sunlight revealed all with the coming day.

The beauty I beheld was both quiet and true,
With stillness in the mists of the morning air.
As the sun sparkled to life in the forming dew,
I knew the stars were still up there somewhere.

What must life be like, so flowing and free?
Being naturally complete in all of its ways,
Unlocking the spirit because it holds a key
In perfect harmony through all of its days?

Walking the twisting turns until nighttime,
Where we came from, we will all shortly go,
Finding rest within our own due time,
Returning to the forest we already know.

Trees

The life of a tree,
Simple and pure,
Growing a life,
Quietly demure.

The lives of the trees
Seeking skyward ways,
Quietly wavering,
Reaching the sun's rays.

Their life in the forest,
A foundation made firm,
Speaking to all of us
By the beauty they affirm.

The lives they all live
In the serenity of silence,
Branching ever upward
In their woodland brilliance.

Changes

All the leaves were long gone
Because the sun couldn't stay,
In the dance across their seasons
Towards a more wintery way.

The trees were standing patiently
Though the birds had long since gone,
Taking a rest from their nests
No longer being bathed in their song.

Creatures were busy scurrying,
Preparing for the future's days,
Getting ready to hibernate
In their life's mysterious ways.

But others ventured onward
Coming out in the twilight,
Remembering the green of their trees
Throughout the snowy night.

Someday they would be back again,
The colorful flowers and trees,
With the warm winds of summer,
So many birds and bees.

And every single night,
The creatures did what they could,
Reassured by those trees
Still standing as they should.

Nature's hard-written rules,
All of its ebbs and flows,
Life emerges to hold on tightly
But then it inevitably goes.

All the plants and animals
Have time in the sunny skies,
To admire their beautiful world
Until their own beauty dies.

Weathermen Fooled Us

Come on, snow!
Where the hell did you go!

Our teeth were clenching for a snowflake drenching.
The cupboards and pantries are now overly full.
An utterly gut-wrenching, snow shovel trenching,
But ultimately, we were all played for the fool!

The weathermen fooled us; we were held by their gaze.
The great storm of all storms to tear things apart—
"You'll be freezing and stranded while stuck in for days!"
But we're all still waiting for the damn thing to start!

Just lies upon lies from those TV guys,
And weathergirls seemingly ditzy and dumb.
I was expecting treacherous snow-filled skies!
Just waiting for my hands and feet to go numb!

But a snowflake falls here or goes down over there
While we huddle in fear of their snowstorm scare,
But it seems a little late to be held by this fate
When the roads are all clear with no snow in the air!

Firefly

I walked across the fields
Under those starry skies,
Their milky effervescence
Illuminating my eyes.

In the pastures of peace,
I saw a single tree,
Under the starlit skies
Like it was beckoning me.

It became clearer as I drew nearer,
Like a twinkle that caught my eye.
In the silence of those stars,
I saw a single firefly.

Glowing as if it was knowing
The sheer majesty of space
With its little show of light
From a humble earthly place.

And then I saw many more,
Inciting and igniting,
Burning with every turn
In their luminous delighting.

They knew the best thing to give,
Though they wouldn't live long,
To reflect beauty while they live
By the light show of their song.

Their torches were all lit,
Beckoning to the skies,
Somehow the stars saw fit
To inspire little fireflies.

Cherry Blossoms

Cherry blossoms were floating,
Flirting with the breeze,
Remembering the past,
Those special times like these.

Warm rains were approaching,
Clouds finding their way,
The stories of our life,
Revealed every day.

Silent fields were whispering,
Sunlight tried to share,
Immortally transfixed,
Compelling us to stare.

Fragile yet ethereal,
Small things awaiting you.
So often overlooked
But always so very true.

Quiet thoughts of peace
Before the racing resumes.
Our life is just a vapor
Which leaves us all too soon.

When we finally understand
To appreciate the experience,
Meanings are understood
Through an earthly deliverance.

It's not easy being human.
Never simple to be true,
So easily overlooked,
The beauty that's before you.

It's there for the taking
As we're tossed and swirled,
Then evermore adoring
Like a whole new world.

The Truth

What would I do?
If I could talk to the world
To its darkest depths
As their dreams unfold?

When their life was troubled
And they felt so weak,
No solutions apparent
When their future seemed bleak.

What would I do?
If I could speak my mind
Across the face of the globe
To my own humankind?

It would be about the Truth
To stimulate light,
Little seeds for their garden
Which would grow just right.

About the joys of life,
The finality of death,
And those spiritual sparkles
To treasure each breath.

Encouraging patience,
The humility of self,
Leaving pride behind
To put it back on its shelf.

Towards the greater things
Much larger than ourselves,
Abandoning the others
Who only consider themselves.

What would I do?
If I were in this position…
Could I improve this place?
For a positive transition…

Indifference

Anger,
Indifference,
The preference
Of difference.

Inference
Of ignorance,
Persistence
In resistance.

No deliverance
Of significance,
Irreverence
Of experience.

No subsistence
For existence
From the anger,
Of indifference.

"MY POEMS ARE LIKE LITTLE AUTONOMOUS ROBOTS THAT I SET FREE TO SPEAK TO PEOPLE'S HEARTS AND MINDS" . "TRUE LOVE REQUIRES A LOVE OF THE TRUTH, AND YOUR ACTIONS PROVIDE THE PROOF"

Hallucinations

Fragmentations of reorganizations,
The willingness to launch a different play.
Elucidations of those interpretations,
Trying to make the pretty colors stay.

Finding the new beats it eventually meets
As the heart hears the spirit far below its love
In becoming replete against its defeats
When the light shines through from so far above.

Just hallucinations or my machinations?
Maybe something that was always meant to stay
In the salutations for our new generations
Because of the artwork that would come into play.

From the deepest parts of my very being,
Those wires and circuits are so hard at work,
Creating a renaissance of my expectations,
Continuing to build with my all-knowing smirk.

Hourglass

Life is the essence
But love makes a way,
Being free to breathe
Then wanting to stay.

Thoughts of our being
Reflecting the mind,
Searching endlessly
For what we might find.

Time progresses,
Experience fills
Sands of the hourglass
Mortality wills.

A fleeting sunshine
And a warmer day
Isn't out of reach
While life has its say.

Fearing aggravation,
Complacency kills,
Draining those sands
That some love refills.

Watch it all spilling,
Your hourglass life.
Refill while you can
To smother the strife.

Sift indecision
The crystalline grains.
Sandcastles can live
While your time remains.

Walk on the beaches
And live on those sands,
Embracing the texture
As it's held in your hands.

Voltage

Like an unearthly arcing and sparking,
I could hear a slight crackling in my ears.
An energetic angelic harkening
Beyond our human doubts and fears.

Electromagnetic radiations
In transmissions just for me,
Intergalactic interpretations
As far as my mind could see.

Constellations of reconciliation
Like the brightest of meteor showers,
A universal remediation
By their strong electrical powers.

Those harmonic oscillations
Like a song meant to set me free,
By their luminary vibrations
As the pathway for things to be.

They were blinking and twinkling
As if they were all winking at me!
Saying "We're gonna electrify you
We're going to be setting you free...

"And we're always going to stay with you.
That future is so ever near,
Like a little bird on your shoulder
So we can tweet it all in your ear...

"The only thing that we'll ask of you
Is to always continue this fight,
To illuminate the many shadows
Dispersing them away with our light."

Higher and higher towards the heavens,
The swirly twirling stars at night,
And the teaching of life in real love,
By the powers of their voltage and light.

The wuthering heights,
Those lonely nights,
Like the fight of all fights
Being rescued by those lights.

Like a spark against the darkness,
A measure of electricity,
There's no need to insulate
A little high voltage for me!

Transparency uncovers
While transcending all the blame,
Then tranquility surrenders
To never again be the same!

In our human evolution,
Singularity is drawing near.
It's time for a revolution
To speak without any fear…

Mirrors

Flat-screen television on the wall,
Who's the fairest of them all?
iPhone and Android in my hand,
Who's the happiest in all the land?

Delicate tablet on my lap,
Show me this world's darkest trap.
Screens of glory from dreams of old,
Display the stories as they unfold.

Computer latency in networks of speed,
Through webs of complacency in filling our need.
Going to the reaches and touching the edges,
As we silently watch from behind our own hedges.

Snow White's dreams of her broken screens,
In dark despair from their disrepair,
The electrons divine as the circuitry defines
The data stream binds as it grabs our minds.

A liquid crystal necromancy so very clear,
A modern-day enoptromancy embroiled in fear,
Mirror, mirror across the webbed wall,
Tell me which screen is the best of all...

What's It Worth?

Just what is anyone's poem worth?
As if it were anything new—
Perhaps only a cup of coffee,
Or maybe even a beer or two.

Just what are anyone's thoughts worth?
From such a humble and lowly place,
When we dream beyond our lifetimes,
As we stare off into space.

Just what is anyone's soul worth?
As their spirit maintains its hold,
Providing light amid the darkness,
Expressing truth that had never been told.

Just what are anyone's dreams worth?
To follow their heart's closest leaning,
Overcoming that innermost frailty
For a greater emotional meaning.

Reflective depths within our memories,
Those utter losses beyond our control.
The many dances across humanity,
The special things that have made us whole.

We're only fleeting incarnations
As the sum of our aspirations.
Imprisoned through expectations
But then freed by our creations.

Just what is anyone's life worth?
The trials we've endured so well,
Climbing our mountains of challenge
While the others eventually fell.

Just what are anyone's efforts worth?
As we engage in this daily fight,
Because that battle is everlasting,
And that's why I continue to write.

Preemptive Paranoia

In the shadows of confinement,
By the shutters holding fast,
With a little more refinement,
Until the dangers finally passed.

Preemptive paranoia,
By a precedence of dread,
Flamboyant inner poison,
Creativity is dead.

Suspicions of the lighter
With a brighter point of view
Must be locked down even tighter
Until there's nothing left to do.

Try to lead that horse to water,
Trying to force a mind to drink,
But those words will only falter
In the way you choose to think.

Preemptive paranoia,
For the things you do not know,
Like a stunted-down sequoia
For a tree that couldn't grow.

As a light shows in the window,
Let the haze obscure the glass,
With new visions stuck in limbo
While the narrowing holds fast.

By the worldliness of worries,
Evil eyes or inner selves,
As the heart rate starts to hurry,
With the books torn from the shelves.

In the cage of no surprises,
Just a fallacy of free,
The questioning arises,
Then, to be or not to be.

Mirrored Masks

Like a carefully blown bubble in search of a pin,
Hiding the old rubble of the dark places we've been,
Or a superficial smile with no hopes of support
From a safe hiding mask, behind that last resort.

Sometimes covering pain to create a better place
Or fleeing in vain while wearing a happier face,
Holding on to a remnant that no one can steal,
Showing the superfluous to protect what is real.

What was ventured and what was gained,
Becoming indentured slaves of things we attained.
Behind a mask of mirrors, many fractures at its best
A brittle glass full of cracks, failing the final test.

Climbing rotten ladders to where we deserve to be,
Ascending the broken rungs as if no one can see,
Or by flagrantly projecting our hollow increase,
But hiding a dead life inside, devoid of any peace.

Plumb-Crazy Purple

My momma said, "Don't buy a muscle car!
It'll kill you and leave you for dead!
You don't need to act like some movie star."
This is what my momma had said.

"You shouldn't be living so carefree.
They're too flashy and boisterously loud.
Be a good little son and don't strain me.
Just keep making your own momma proud.

"Those fast cars are so diabolical.
It's no good if you can't survive.
Just get something more economical,
Like a nice little Toyota to drive...

"Going slowly, in a four-door family car,
Or you'll wrap yourself around a tree!"
But I'd dreamed of driving a Challenger,
So it was a plumb-crazy purple one for me!

Playhouses

In the dreams of our youthful ambitions,
The energy that we all used to have,
The aspirations of all those inspirations
And those things we could never quite have.

The quietness of an entire lifetime,
The creativity that wanted to take control,
The simplistic stupidity of our dreams,
The little things we think will make us whole.

But there's always merit in your lowly desires.
It's the only spark that makes us alive,
Letting the heart do what it aspires
So that hopefulness always survives...

I know this all too very well,
Being such a magnificent dreamer myself.
The many playhouses within our mind
Were never meant to play all by themself.

Elusivity

That ever-elusive female,
Something I write about occasionally,
Like a dash just past the forbidden
In a goal perused so aimlessly.

Like a flash beyond the pan
As a target that is never-ending,
In a life of mediocrity
For a status that's worth defending.

In a world of hurt and delusion,
Real life somehow always resists.
Some say it's just a delusion,
But I believe that it still exists...

Something far past the ethereal
In the very essence of what's romantic,
Like it was all just meant to be so.
I'd like something really fantastic.

Sing a Song

All of the things that you'd hoped for...
Trying to see the sun through the rain,
Feeling the essence of your displacement,
Realizing that many of your endeavors were in vain.

As we do the dance with each new chance,
Like a roll of the dice could ever suffice,
As if our stance would ever lead to romance,
Like a block of ice could ever be that nice...

In the emergencies of your urgency,
The inner drives that help you survive..
An S.O.S. amid your complacency,
Just wanting to get above the water to stay alive.

In the beautiful meadows of the sun's quiet grace,
The sort of things that we've hoped for so long.
In the simplicity of then simply living,
For some new inspiration to sing a song.

Sleep On It

It was just a little beyond belief,
The strange things that I saw.
After a night of restful sleep,
I awoke to this optical flaw...

I went outside to be in the sun,
Or go for a swim and have some fun.
But I was in for a real big surprise:
Something was wrong with my sleepy eyes.

Cats were acting like dogs,
And the dogs all looked like cats.
I did see some kids playing football,
But they were using baseball bats!

The trees were glowing kind of purple,
The grass was anything but green.
A kaleidoscope of confusion,
The strangest things I've ever seen...

I wasn't quite sure what to make of it,
Like those fish floating in the air.
I was contemplating my sanity,
While all I could do was stare.

Or the roads that seemed like licorice,
And that person with a propeller cap.
I could swear the buildings were all gumdrops,
I even thought I saw the Cat in the Hat.

And the sun was up there talking,
Saying it was too hot in its room!
An unbelievable illusion.
I hoped it would be ending soon.

Then suddenly a bark!
It kind of went through my head.
It still seemed a little dark.
Hey! I was still in my bed...

It was that little pet dog of mine,
Reminding me of its feeding time.

Things strange as they were seeming,
The weirdest place I'd ever been,
It was because I was still dreaming.
So much for sleeping in...

Cathetometer   Buttery   Ironwort

Arboricolous

Increscent   Hexaemeron

Tirailleur   Vergence   Storge

Conation   Zenocentric

Atticism   Jailage   Polylemma

Vulnerose

Idiologism   Ecophobia   Ceilometer

Antimetathesis

Complacency   Consideration   Memories

Bigfoot   Chickens rule

Thoughtfulness   Awe   Humor

Roller skates   Time travel

Werewolf

New Year's Resolutions...

It was a New Year's resolution,
A humanitarian solution,
To somehow better my life
Avoiding the past year's strife.

To finally become just a little more fit
By getting on up to get on with it.
No longer feeling quite so lazy,
No more seemingly quite so crazy.

No longer watching a dull TV screen,
Deadened by the drama of shows I'd seen.
With no more munchies to eat in the dark,
But rather some water for a walk in the park.

Holding the doors for the people I see,
Always washing my hands after I pee.
Being polite to say *thank you so much*.
As for all my old friends, I'll get in touch.

Renounce bad habits like beer and smokes
And only ever telling the most tasteful jokes.
Maybe even trying to read a few books,
Release all the fish that I catch on my hooks.

Oh! Washing my car and waxing it too,
My God, there's gonna be a lot to do
Towards the newest year as I've resolved,
Like a perfect person who's truly evolved.

And certainly trying to lose some weight
For a lighter life in a streamlined state,
Then trying to be a bit more happy than sad
And attempting to do more good than bad.

There are many resolves as the planet revolves,
The ascension of hope and the problems it solves.
But in next year's life, the truth always shows.
Will we meet those goals? Who the hell knows?

Hurt in the Yurt

I was eating some yogurt in my yurt
Outside of the edge of town,
Having recently been hurt
When my bicycle had tumbled down.

It's not so easy to play the hippie
For a life that's serene and pure.
That slope can be a little bit slippy
But it's still pretty groovy for sure.

Abandoning my business suits
To wear a headband in their place
As I chased down my inner fruits
While staring off into outer space.

Would I find a revelation in nothing?
Somehow scoring just a little bit more?
Or was I really only just bluffing
With those tie-die shirts that I wore...

(and yes I meant tie-die)

Rubber Shoes

I really like those rubber shoes,
The *Crocs* with socks I often use.

Not so stylish
But nice for sure,
As the mud awaits
When you step out the door.

I look a little funny
But sorry, that's me.
A well-dressed man?
Well, he isn't me!

I do have nice shoes
That I seldom use,
For I wear them out
From my daily abuse.

I prefer the rubber,
Resilient and all,
Good-gripping soles
So I seldom fall.

When they need shined
So they're clean and slick,
A little motor oil
Always does the trick!

There's no need to fret
When they're muddy and wet
Because a warm, sunny day
Makes them dry out okay.

In those piles of manure
Or those puddles of slime,
I wear those rubber shoes
Almost all the time…

Ginger-Head

I'd almost completely missed him
As I walked on out the door—
That little man in a baggie
Whatever he'd been placed there for...

Just sitting alone on the counter
Being a little bit out of place
And looking rather lonely
With that icing all over his face.

I'm a little bit of a rookie
About the makings of a cookie,
But he smelled like gingerbread
Unless it was all just in my head.

They were giving them out free!
And who would have ever thought
But that treat somehow escaped me!
Because I completely forgot!

Then I went on about my business,
Driving away to my favorite stores,
But next time I see one of these,
I'll have to see if they have any more...

Water Into Wine

Water, water, everywhere,
But not a drop to drink,
For I preferred my bottled water.
Rather than the kitchen sink!

It's not from my idiosyncrasy,
But rather for making some wine, you see,
And not that I needed that much for me.
It was for my homemade wine-making spree!

I've always hated that nasty chlorine;
It doesn't fit into the wine-making scene.
Chemicals in water don't make it clean,
Like that fluoride sister of toxic fluorine.

I simply don't care for their metallic taste,
Lest my brilliant flavors become displaced
For a fermented failure that would be disgraced.
So, I make all my wines very naturally based!

For a purer form of what will be in store,
A natural experience with every pour.
In the mouthfeel of body, you can't ignore
For an organic wine that you can adore!

And on this hobby, I've spent some time,
Tweaking the variables I need to refine
To produce my very own product line
From my newest skill,
        Of turning water into wine…

Dogecoin Miner

Like bite-sized Bitcoins,
The Dogecoins were mined,
A digital luminescence
As the gold was refined.

Electricity was arcing
As graphics cards drilled,
The Doges were barking
And the ASICs were thrilled.

By themes and memes
In fluorescent flair,
The coins ran wild
As they dropped from the air.

Those Dogecoin miners
By the sweat of their brow
Created such currency
For a coin that's WOW!

Horrifyingly Orange

My hair was horrifyingly orange!
After dyeing it to audition for a play,
Like a burnt sweet potato casserole
Or a Halloween pumpkin puree!

Yes, I kind of looked a little strange,
Perhaps colored too much like some fruits,
But we endure many trials of styles
When entertaining theatrical pursuits…

Hopefully with the cold stage light,
My colors would blaze a whole new way,
Most artistic, fashionable, and bright
So that orange would save my day.

There was a glint in the director's eye,
Then my color turned it into a stare.
Perhaps next time I should use less dye
So I can have more manageable hair.

Banana Bread

When the bananas came home, fresh from the store,
The whole bunch thought, "Hey this is neat!
We will be placed in a bowl of the greatest privilege
Overlooking the shopper's favorite seat!

"They must value our yellowed beauty
More than any other fruit that they might meet,
For we were carefully grown in the deepest jungles
With a wild flavor most delicate and sweet."

But as time went by, they weren't paid any mind.
The humans ate the lesser fruit they would find,
Busy devouring potato chips as if they were a big treat
And sugar-laced impostors who weren't naturally sweet.

Then the whole bunch noticed some banana bread
And even what looked like some old banana pie!
Suddenly they realized with a fructose-filled dread—
That's where they would go when they rot and die!

They tried yelling: "Hey humans, please choose us!
What's with all the junk food? What's the big fuss!
You need to eat healthy stuff rather than that tripe.
We are here in our prime for you, healthy and ripe."

But the people never heard since bananas can't speak.
The outlook from their overlook now looked very bleak.
From beauty to oblivion as the bowl on the counter spins,
Through time the age of the enzymes invariably wins.

And just what of a banana's life could ever be said,
But when it gets old, you can use it to make bread.
Since we can't hear them, we don't know if they cry,
So you can always use them all for a new banana pie…

PART TWO:
family and friends

Just Another Mother's Day

It's just another Mother's Day,
So what's the big deal?
But you only have one mother.
Consider how she must feel...

Your mother will always love you
To the very day that she dies.
That's why she took care of you,
That's why she always tries.

Raising you up through trials,
Trembling within each fight,
Guiding you in good directions,
Trying to teach you what was right.

She will always think of you,
This should come as no surprise.
It's why she wants to hug you,
And that's why she cries.

Your mother was the only one
Who held you from the start.
In her life's greatest story,
You'll always play a part.

The one who always remembers
That first look in your eyes—
With small hands and feet,
And that's why she sighs.

But she won't always be there
Because life never lets us stay—
Something you need to remember
On the next Mother's Day.

Snowballs

There was a winter's chill
But we all still had fun,
sledding down the hill
in the clear winter sun.

It was a cold day of play,
Our mittens stuck to the sleds,
And a frantic snowball fray
With woolen caps on our heads.

As we all slipped and slid,
Never really knowing
How nice it was being a kid
In our yard as it was snowing.

And then as we grew older,
Winter was never the same.
Each year seemed a little colder,
Reliving our childhood game.

Home

The places that we all come from,
The space that we left in vain,
Through the turbulence of inconvenience,
The very faces we return to again.

For just a little bit of security,
Some surety, in the face of our demise,
Remembering our yesterdays...
Those calming memories before our eyes.

A place that was ever accepting,
Where you would never feel alone,
In the faces of so many connections,
That place that you could always call home.

For just a little bit of stability,
An anchored island against any storms,
In the face of life's insecurities,
It's the very beginning that always transforms...

Just Another Father's Day

It's just another Father's Day,
So, what's the big deal?
Well perhaps you should ask him.
Hey! Is this thing for real?

Well, I did help to raise you,
And that's just the start.
Though your mom did so very much,
I also played my own part.

I tried so hard to guide you
In a very deliberate way
With a fatherly type of compass
To give you some wisdom every day.

As a means of greater stability,
Like a hard metal that cannot bend,
A foundation for your future surety,
Something I was always ready to defend.

This is what fathers were made for,
How they all are supposed to be—
Through love by a tougher patience
In hopes that you would always live free.

And always focused on security,
So your house could become a home,
Carefully maintaining that framework,
So you would never have to feel alone.

Last Thanksgiving

It was a day like so many others,
The times we were among our friends,
Those holidays that we're now living,
Until our own life eventually ends.

Always remembering our parents,
Since they meant so much to us,
And all the others that are now long gone,
The many things that we used to discuss.

As if it was merely a family gathering,
Or could it be just a little bit more,
When you've seen the brevity of life,
With no more knocks upon your door.

And never forget during the holidays
That our mortality is never forgiving,
In God's mysterious ways,
It could always be the last Thanksgiving.

Funeral For a Son

It all seemed so surreal,
Like a nightmare while I was awake.
A dream with no hopes of dissipating,
Although it was a bad dream.
It wasn't.

As the minutes ticked away,
The appointed time would come.
His time.
My time.
Our time before he would be removed,
Never to be seen again,
Or heard,
Forcefully relegated to my memories.
Only in my thoughts.
No hopes whatsoever.
As his flesh rots away in its new absence of life,
Underground,
In the dark,
Forever.
But there's still time here
In this lit room, with him right here,
So close
But worlds apart,
Just a memory that I can still see.
Friends coming to see all of us,
Offering their condolence and support.
But soon the viewing will be over,
The funeral home will close,
The doors will be shut,
All the lights will be turned off,
And I will have to go home.
A deadened home,
Devoid of the future I had envisioned.
Somehow lifeless,
Just like him.

Promise

Great ice castles were made,
Many snowmen were built,
But that memory would fade
Under Grandmother's quilt.

In their youth, all was new.
With vigor, they'd run,
But eventually, they grew
Out of childhood's fun.

It's that way for each of us
As we grow and learn.
Fun is now superfluous
With life cold and stern.

We should strive to make a way
To revisit the joys of our past,
See new promises every day
So that our youth will always last.

Laboratory
Temporal
Nonremittal
Understanding
Illustrate
Sequence
Appoint
Explosion
Strong
Fuss
Build
Inesive
Anicular
Monadism
Tippet
Deorsumversion
Theriac
Modulo
Gauntlet

The Mothers of Our Past

The mothers of our past,
We thought they'd always last,
But they had to leave us
Though they never wanted to.
Then,
We didn't know what to do.

Out of a young girl's dreams,
So long ago it now seems,
She brought forth your life.
Then the world made her go away,
Even though she struggled to stay.

All the books she once read,
The songs she sang,
The things she said.
A large part of what your world was
Now singing only in your past
But a part of you that will always last.

And she loved you until the day she died,
As inside she remembered and cried,
It's just another hard part of our life,
But the spark in that young girl's dreams,
Is now yours and what motherhood means.

*"Through the dreams of a young girl to be a mother and a wife,
you were once created and brought into this life." - Kirke Wise*

Beth Ann

In the depths of a distant galaxy,
Far beyond our understanding,
They discussed life's inconsistencies,
The very things that the truth was demanding.

For our world that was so out of balance,
In a place of unnecessary fear,
It would just take a bit of encouragement,
A simple person who could bring some more cheer.

And she would excel at all those wonderings,
To bring a brightness against their old strife,
For the children of our future's enlightenment,
A fond spot in the memories of their lives.

A person of some understanding
At the whims of an astral commanding.
This is what the stars were demanding,
Someone who was totally outstanding.

For the sparkle of a true effervescence,
The clear simplicity of her inner essence,
Changing hearts with her humble presence,
Like a star in the glory of its fluorescence.

And the world would eventually see her,
It was all just a part of their plan,
For someone who was meant to be here,
And her name would be called Beth Ann...

Scientific

Scientific symbols,
Batteries and lights,
Caught a young boy's mind
Through his days and nights.

Beakers and loudspeakers,
With the tubes all aglow,
Radio circuitry,
All the things he would know.

In a science of wonder
With rules to defend,
Creations to find,
A vision to ascend.

Magnetic fragments,
The microscope slides,
From our very own sun
There's no place to hide.

Shining a light,
Minds make their way,
Dreaming of meanings
With every new day.

Science!

That's where it's at,
New worlds to discover.
A brightly lit future,
As facts would uncover.

Not blinded by time,
But a quest for the truth,
Carefully analyzing,
The scientific proof.

By the liters and meters,
Stained glass with the gas,
Through beakers and speakers,
His mind's atomic mass.

Transcending transformations,
Not so well behaved.
Finding new paths,
On roads unpaved.

Making many garden stones,
And other works of art.
Daring the unknowns,
In trying to do his part.

And the science will live on,
Because I'm far worse.
I swirl all those dreams,
Of the Wise family curse.

Mother's Day

Once again, it's Mother's Day,
A special time every year,
Something to never take lightly,
Being earned with every tear.

No mother should ever feel lonely.
It's such a simple thing.
She's the one and only
Who made you laugh whenever she'd sing.

Remembering the mothers of our past,
Giving us guidance that was just right.
Their wisdom will eternally last,
Living their jobs every day and night.

It's for all the things that you've done,
Bruises and cuts that were cared for,
Those many battles patiently won,
That's what mothers were made for.

In a way, no one else could ever do
A great job was completed by you!
Through it all, you found a way,
That job of tough love with little pay.

Raising them up through every birthday,
What greater thing could anyone say?
Well, there is a great deal more,
But the least I can say is:
            Have a happy Mother's Day!

Ideal Holiday

The ideal holiday is for a few,
Each with our different life.
Others have little left to do,
Being cut by this world's knife.

Some lost their loved ones,
Having nothing left to say.
A spouse, daughters, or sons,
Remembering parents that day.

Many lives are just broken,
Things didn't quite work out.
The cruel world has spoken,
Leaving only fear and doubt.

Life within the lonely void,
Making holidays deeply blue.
With the celebrations to avoid,
Know that we care about you.

And just please remember this:
Through life's stormy weather,
Coping when things are amiss,
We all travel this life together.

Atomic Swing

Though it was old and battered,
It had never been fixed.
As if a swing should ever matter,
The calming charms it transfixed.

The simple joys of its motion
As the world raced around.
Revisiting carefree times,
Back and forth, up and down.

Of the many things we could hope to aspire,
By the scenes of those dreams in the depths of our minds.
Imaginations in motion to be lit on fire,
The tranquility of treasures you can easily find...

One of the simplest things that man has made,
Is to simply be able to swing in the shade.
Generations have seen it and swung on its course,
From childhoods, marriages, deaths, and divorce.

Over the span of the plans of a hundred years,
The ambitions and hopes against fears of the tears.
Like a peaceful garden inside your life,
Is there really a chance to have such a thing?

But I saw fit to give it life once more,
And now it's known as the Atomic Swing...

Orphans

We will all become orphans.
It's very sad yet true.
Suddenly, we're left alone,
Not knowing what to do.

Life does go on,
But not as it should,
Because you will miss them
When they are gone for good.

Like my mother once said,
She might not be able to stay.
I know that she wanted to,
But she didn't manage to find a way.

And I watched my father
As he took his very last breath,
Flipping the switch of his dreams,
From life going into death.

And we were there for them,
To help them both go,
Reconciling our divisions,
So that they would finally know.

Not a chance that everyone gets,
But I did, perhaps to see,
So that I could relate some of this
To you, from within me.

Someday it will happen,
You'll never be the same.
Realize the present value.
Instead of ignoring future pain.

Suddenly you'll be lost
In realizing that you're alone
With a non-redeemable cost,
When you no longer have a home.

And as this life goes on,
Yours will go on too.
Let your own orphans know
So, they'll know what to do…

Little Fortress

The little boy's fort was magical inside,
A place he could run to every day,
With spaces to dream and places to hide
In the fort he built as a spot to play.

The little boy's fort had blankets so thick
They could keep out monsters, dragons, and such,
Carefully considering the materials he'd pick,
The strongest of forts was never too much.

The little boy's fort was his pride and joy,
A castle he built by his very own hands,
A great work of art and not just a toy.
He commanded it all like a fort demands.

The little boy's dreams all came into play
As creation flourished from his childlike skill.
Bigger and better they'd become someday.
Do you think he can do it? I just bet he will.

Christmas Eve

The kids were restless and excited.
It was finally now Christmas Eve.
Their parents were acting a little funny,
Like they had something up their sleeve.

They got to see Grandma and Grandpa
Having lots of fun earlier in the day,
But now for the magical night's sleep,
And then tomorrow presents and play!

Through the many years, they all grew,
And someday they would be the adults,
Trying their best to provide the same way,
Regardless of their shortcomings or faults.

These things are given within our lives,
The small child's innocent awe and elation,
Then with reflection doing the best we can,
Remembering the magic as our inspiration.

"Fishing for rhymes within the depth of our minds."

(Photo by: Jodie Beabout)

Lori Jean

In the deepest mists of a quiet forest,
From the serenity of its oldest trees,
Came a singular song and colorful chorus
To let Mother Nature do as she pleased.

Spreading light in this world among the living
With an understanding of our own inner minds,
A celebration of nature's humble thanksgiving,
To show the best that its starlight defines.

Over the rolling hills of budding flowers
And the serenity of its peaceful ponds,
The delicate lives of its lowly animals,
In the ways that nature always responds.

There was a care in the air of understanding
From those people who were meant to be,
Demanding their love, notwithstanding,
Because they'd naturally cared to see.

In the art of each part among the plants
And the intricacies of their short lives,
Those very things that we should all see,
To grasp the beauty which always survives.

Through the careful insight of an artist's delight,
To show the serenity of all that was seen
With a magical ability to display that light.
There would come an artist named Lori Jean.

Kathleen Marie

Sometimes the world seems silent
For any hopes that it has to bring,
When all that's offered is confusion,
As if it's devoid of almost everything.

When the children are trying to grow up,
Striving to find their own special place,
And so often wanting to give it all up,
When the past comes to slap them in the face.

Not every childhood is like a fairy tale,
No family is as perfect as it should be.
Sometimes, as if it was destined to fail,
Like a prisoner with no way to be set free.

Without those little spots of brightness
And somehow devoid of any true caring,
Without those examples of forthrightness,
To feel like a misfit beyond any repairing.

And they would need a little something more,
A genuine dose of some caring and sharing.
The sorts of simple things that kids hope for,
A sense of family that didn't need repairing.

And with some guidance as a steadfast light,
In patience, to always show what was right,
With no more fears of malevolence or spite,
So there would be no more reasons to fight.

There would be someone in that corner with them,
Trying her best to help them to find their way,
With true empathy and compassion to show them,
To instill their hopes toward a much brighter day.

In playing her part from a teacher's heart
To bring out the better and abandon the worse,
So her students could see what it was to break free
And walk away from their circumstantial curse.

Her guidance would take a place in their memories.
Was there any chance that they'd come to see?
For a special space in their own life's treasuries
As they would come to love Kathleen Marie.

90

PART THREE:
being human

Low-skilled

Low-skilled writers with the courage
Started with something to say
Because they had to see a change
And wanted to make a better way.

Low-skilled poets with resolve
Challenged their own world's curse.
They fought by weapons of words,
Waging battles with their careful verse.

Low-skilled painters with a purpose
Saw sunlight in a different scene.
They wanted a world full of colors
For a life that was more serene.

Low-skilled sculptors with feeling
Tried to express it all with their hand
As models of the things to come,
New worlds where they would stand.

Low-skilled potters with pride
Slowly made their visions real
In the vessels of our existence
That were turned by their wheel.

Low-skilled weavers with patience,
Using threads cut by a knife,
Covered all our weaknesses,
Making the tapestries of life.

Low-skilled musicians in harmony,
Hearing clearer words to sing,
With rhythms against disruption
To remove the world's sharpest sting.

Low-skilled dreamers with no vision
Would someday see a brand-new thing
By dreaming like a mere child
A whole new world they would bring.

Low-skilled craftsman with work
Reshaped this all from the start,
Building a new civilization
Empowering the greatest part.

Low-skilled people like all of us
Kept improving as a matter of will,
And through that perseverance,
They gradually increased their skill.

Winter

From the many seasons of our life,
Those very first lessons about love,
Just trying to learn how to survive
The occasional brushes with hate.

When those special people have passed
As we're once again alone in the world,
In a fairy tale that could never last,
It always seems to end with our winter…

Like the melodies of symphonies
With their entrancing ups and downs,
So captivating while you can listen…
As if our lives were in those very sounds.

With every new cycle of the moonlight,
The warmest greetings of each bright sun,
There's space to run, laugh, and play,
The times to enjoy as you're having fun.

The shortest seasons to remember
Because they never come again,
In the melancholy cycle of existence
With its utter triumphs of pain.

By the first glimmers of springtime,
Reaching for the stars untold,
Not so very far from the divine
As the brightness of life unfolds.

In the coming summer of enchantment
When you could do as you pleased,
Only warmer, clearer, and brighter
Where things could never have freezed.

Then, in the certain approach of autumntime,
As the colorful leaves all fall to the ground,
In the raining winds of a whirling change,
That summertime could no longer be found.

The special things we've experienced,
So many different places,
The look on your loved ones' faces,
In the stories of our human races.

Still running as it becomes tiring
Toward the season of disparities,
As every day a bit more is taken away
And then all that's left are the memories.

Reflections

It seemed so very quiet,
Just sitting in my backyard,
Considering the stuff of life,
Wondering why it's so hard.

Dimly lit as the darkness engulfed,
I wondered at the moon so far above.
Was it there to answer the sunshine?
Or perhaps to let us fall in love?

The harshness of each day's fight
Being followed by its softer light,
A time to contemplate and reflect
About life and the love we neglect.

Quietly marking our life's journeys
A silent witness up in the air,
With much softer realizations,
If we only listen to its care.

Inanely Insane

Lonely,   Looking for the sunlight of different days,
Alone,   Grasping for pathways in different ways,
Inane,   Seeking connections against the division,
Unknown.   To realize those visions of your own revision.

Just what was it that you were meant to be?
Those fires never lit so you could be free.

Unbalanced – not favoring,
Misplaced – and wavering…
Unsteady yet still by your strength of will.
Have you suffered enough yet to have your fill?

Faulted – halted,
Insinuated – insulted!
Seeking in silence and sensing the divides,
Fleeing ambivalence as your fate decides.

Stinking -- shrinking,
Wasted – yet still thinking…
I want you to stay for a better way,
To carefully consider the dynamics at play.

If magic could speak it would surely say,
"Be real right now and exist for today!
Living clear and true while being just you!
Because that's what we were supposed to do…"

And just who is there to really blame
As we're twisted and twirled within this world,
Somewhere surreal, and most surely insane,
But the more we give, the greater we'll gain.

A paradox of irony as the opposites attract,
In a life that despairingly looks for its match,
Running on the wheels of just what it feels,
Opening the letters that circumstance unseals.

Trying to find the order from deep within,
Striving to balance those needs against sin,
Remembering the places, you've already been,
To revisit that base as you finally begin…

Changes

If you want your life to change,
First, you must change your life.
Consolidating your happiness
Will eliminate countless strife.

If you want things to be different,
You will have to forge them anew.
To understand the course correction
Be mindful of each little clue.

If you want it to flow naturally,
Follow what works best.
As a river stays in its proper place.
You too will pass that test.

Thoughts

I only wanted to live a carefree life,
Just happy in the love that I'd found,
Trying my best to surpass all the rest,
But then, there was no more of that around.

Just the simplistic story of a lifetime,
So many things wasted along the way,
The various mistakes that I'd made,
Those truths that I was so hesitant to say.

Like the misfires of a broken engine
With no spark to ignite its fires,
Completely out of life's true timing
Only the duds of what a heart desires.

These were the remnants of memories,
Things I'd never again hope to find.
Just the ashes of a burned-out landscape
With those few remaining thoughts of mine.

I suppose that it never hurts to try
To somehow experience the divine,
But it was a dream that was ultimately shattered,
Leaving only those thoughts of mine…

Darkest Fears

Your darkest fears,
A life of regrets.
A story of tears,
Time never forgets.

Daylight for another,
While you're still dark.
Emotions smother,
You missed the mark.

And this world turns,
While desire spins.
Humanity yearns,
But only chance wins.

Violently mixed,
Beaten by life.
Utterly vexed,
Cut with a knife.

Screaming in quiet,
Grasping unknowns.
Needfully silent,
Graves full of bones.

Wasted by the way,
Deserted roads.
What can we say?
Life's overloads.

And can we make it?
Those who have lost,
Ever admitting
Such a great cost.

I don't know for sure,
But please still try,
For hope is the cure
Before we die.

Bookshelves

Dead - unsaid,
Books of words.
Unspoken,
Never read...

Volumes shut,
Choices brittle,
Pages sticking,
Chances little.

Paragraphs the same,
Binding the pages,
Games of crosswords,
On lonely stages.

By the bookshelf,
Between the others,
Unnoticed covers,
Rejected lovers.

Refusing categories,
Refuting fates,
Recycling redundancy,
Rebuttal awaits.

Novels of games,
Unreachable goals,
Darkened pages,
Emptied souls.

Desolate places,
Empty spaces,
Shelves devoid,
On those bookcases.

Mold awaits,
Humidity wins,
Disfiguring fates,
Unresponsive sins.

Real

Unpolished,
But pure.
Unvarnished,
For sure.

Simple thoughts,
Easy words,
Battles fought,
Life's records.

Say what you think,
Relate how you feel,
Just be yourself,
To live in the real.

Dive from that cliff,
Soar with the breeze,
Indifferently differing,
Doing as you please.

Quite unashamed,
And sure of yourself,
Open your books,
Pull them off the shelf.

Fan all the pages,
The chapters flash by,
Your innermost life,
Letting thoughts fly.

You'll be unbound,
Far above mere words,
The sentences of truth,
They all point towards.

You'll feel at home,
Being as you are,
Not having to hide,
A better life by far.

Wasted

Wasted thoughts,
Wasted vision,
Wasted signs,
Lacking precision.

Empty sympathy,
Empty concern,
Empty honesty,
As you'll learn.

Wasted effort,
Wasted words,
Wasted time,
Adjectives and verbs.

Empty meanings,
Empty scars,
Empty hope,
From empty jars.

Wasted connections,
Wasted days,
Wasted forever,
In barren ways.

Empty motives,
Empty hearts,
Empty minds,
In false starts.

Wasted emotions,
Wasted tears,
Wasted away,
Throughout the years.

Empty meaning,
Empty roles,
Empty fields,
Unobtainable goals.

Fallen

In the forest, a tree fell quietly,
Cut apart from its lofty air.
There was no one to hear it,
None were left to care.

Finally reaching the end
With that last-needed breath,
It all became irrelevant now
As he fell into his death.

And some will see the others
Who ventured on before,
In a world apart from our own
As they stepped through life's last door.

Across our worldly timeline,
An eternity we have sought,
For a spirit filled with honesty
By a soul that can't be bought.

Your first love for the truth
This world will try to steal,
Compromising your connection,
Then making you unreal.

Pencils and Papers

There are paper hearts,
Origami dreams,
Through a crinkled life
That's not as it seems.

The faintest of traces
By their pencil's lead
Were left from their life
By a love never read.

Folded up carefully,
Placed in the drawer,
To escape from the light
Never lit anymore.

Then creased until cutting
As it all tears away,
No pencils or paper
Nothing more left to say...

Sunlit visions

Only in my dreams
As the sun breaks the sky,
Like a haunting, it seems,
Before that time, I should die.

Not among those things
That you see while you sleep,
But with eyes wide awake,
So meaningful and deep.

As those visions were rendered,
My own heart surrendered
Past the futility of life
But in the brightness of its light.

Within the stillness of noise
Of our own daily lives,
In some visions of the future
Where hopefulness survives.

The universe responds
As it comes into play,
In making a new way
Where that hope corresponds.

Where nothing was ventured,
Nothing will ever be gained,
With no stories of adventure,
The possibilities were stained.

Though others around might be dying,
I'll always keep on trying,
Because those dreams will keep me flying,
For a life that's beyond denying.

And when it's all said and done,
With sunlit visions far away,
I'll be recalling that time,
Remembering the warmth of its day.

Dandelions

In the fields laid out before me,
Underneath a warm spring sky,
A message from the lowliest of flowers
That I should never let my hopes die.

Towards the promise of a new summer,
The warmth of that sun-filled time,
Knowing the wisdom of nature's cycles
And that most guarded heart of mine...

Considering our human needs,
As I was pulling out those little weeds,
But with their beautiful yellow flowers,
They possessed unearthly powers...

The very colors of give and take
The hues of a serene afternoon,
And the bright sunlight is never fake,
Though our serenity sets so very soon.

Like our own needs among the weeds,
Sprawling as they try to make their way,
Gripping desperately for some sustenance,
Reaching their way toward a fruitful day.

In the calm of a peaceful yard,
Could life really be that hard?
But I knew that I would do just fine,
Because I was going to make,
                    some dandelion wine.

Bipolar

There were voices in my head
Trying to tell me what to do,
Trying to lead the way I think
Like a spiritual coup.

They said I wasn't good enough,
There would never be a way,
As if all would soon be lost.
That's what they would always say.

Like the world was all against me
On my rollercoaster ride,
Uncontrollable ups and downs
With no place that I could hide.

Through the solace of my thoughts,
In the darkness of my dreams,
The many solitary battles,
In the silence of my screams.

When I would gain a foothold,
Like the victory was near,
My thoughts returned to taunt me,
With a voice of doubt and fear.

Then I began to realize
In my battles to be free.
Those voices weren't from another,
But just the other side of me.

Painted Grey

In those still and reflective moments,
From the sobriety of a life's own dream,
Past the tripe of our closely held hype
With some true honesty of self-esteem.

When we were young and beautiful,
Being just the foreshadowing of a lie,
We were so strong and invincible,
But time fades those hopes as they die.

As the flowers seem to lose their color,
A cold world chills the warmth of the sun.
Hopefulness continues to grow smaller,
Right up until you're the only one.

We've got to reach past those fears
And reclaim what is truly ours.
Transcending all of the doubts,
So we can touch our own bright stars.

With a vision that flowers renewal
No longer being just painted grey,
To recreate those earliest dreams
In a much more colorful way.

Green

So, what's the appeal
Of this chlorophyll,
When the meadow is silent
And the grasses are still?

Green is for money,
In the color of greed,
But it also holds flowers
To support nature's need.

In the world all around us
By our sky's lighter blue,
There is much to consider
With a thoughtful hue.

Being green with envy
Or greener through life,
Just stop to then see it
With the flowers so rife.

The grass may seem greener
On that other side
As you tally for takeoff
From your own foolish pride.

Life isn't always
In what can be seen,
But in nature's own way
Just think about the green.

When the Past was Present

When it was all quite different,
In fact, getting better every day,
But that was nothing more
Than a foolish dream, it seems,
As human dynamics came into play.

Because as we rise toward the Heavens,
Attempting our best toward a glorious flight,
Sometimes it all just dissolves
As our former goals are lost from sight...

For it always takes two to tango
In the harmony of a beautiful dance,
Ever ascending much higher
Through the hopefulness of romance.

But the somehow tainted visions,
Those eventual divisions,
Ever descending revisions
By a contrary heart's decisions.

When the past was present,
The dreams that we were holding fast,
Building a treasure of memories,
But they just simply couldn't last...

Little Birdies

I came across a little birdie,
In the shortening of the day,
Chirping enthusiastically
As if I should hear what it had to say.

About how the sunlight felt right,
That winter wouldn't last forever,
Among the fields of various flowers
In the golden rule of the birdies,
          To never ever say never.

We're just little creatures of the light,
Not constrained by any walls,
Yet our own creator knows
Whenever any one of us falls.

For the winter will surely come
As we fly away from the past.
Then we'll take to a newer flight
Once that colder season has passed.

Regaining our place under the stars
As we glide on thoughtful wings,
Deeper than you may understand
In the complex songs that nature sings.

For nothing that was ever covered
Shall be able to remain hidden,
Consciousness so very close to you
If you're only willing to listen…

Those simple little birdies
As they go about their tasks,
A small part of something much greater,
Cycles of life that eternally last.

And all around this world
In every single place,
Creation tries to speak to you
Toward a truth you need to embrace.

Rocket

I have an ideal
About the vibrancy of our lives,
In the power of possibilities
And the intention that survives.

Chances never taken,
Opportunities missed,
Rebirth forsaken,
Enlightenment dismissed...

But I'm not like that—
I can see those lights above,
The stars shining wistfully
In the very essence of human love.

Like a worn-out fairy tale
But with some power still in it,
Piercing beyond that uncertain veil,
And somehow,
I still believe in it...

In the most elementary trajectory
To simply shoot on over the moon,
Daring past a life of rejections,
Reflections of the universe coming soon

In a different place of our space,
Filled with the newness of hopeful vision,
Past the horizons of darker thoughts,
To meet the stars in a whole new visitation.

Where the lights are so very bright
And the spirit is in control of the senses.
As you win, you no longer need to fight;
Power is often given to the defenseless.

In the seeming futility of humility,
Just yearning for those simple things,
All you must do is start the countdown
For the power that a hopeful rocket brings.

That Is

That is to be loved
Among the things of your life—
The ups and downs
And all-arounds,
Even during your strife.

That is to be remembered,
The tougher times that you've faced—
In your journey out the other side
With new truths that you embraced.

That is to be cherished,
Those special times that you've had—
From love and joy with peaceful dreams
When nothing could ever go bad.

That is to be considered,
The changing states within our lives—
But everything rises in a heart that's clear
Where hopefulness survives.

That is to be alive,
What life has chosen to provide—
Slowly learning through wisdom
With no longer any reason to hide.

That is to say,
There isn't any other way—
And all the good memories you can make
Aren't something that anyone can take…

Little Secret

I'll tell you a little secret:
I've written a few things.
At first, scared to publish
From the scrutiny it brings,

But I could see beyond that
As written on everyone's face.
We are all just merely humans,
All existing within this place.

To each their own yet the others,
Humanity demands that we feel,
Never forgetting those struggles,
Ascending until we become real.

I'll tell you something more
Because I stand in a room of light:
You should step through that door
So you understand what is right…

The Road

I've been staring at the wall,
Thinking about the things that could have been
Just waiting
To once again become free.

Wondering about the possibilities,
The never-ending stories of life,
Until they all seem to hit the wall.
What's in store for me now?

The paths we wander aimlessly,
The balance that we decide,
The very windows from our soul,
The places that we choose to hide.

The road so heavily traveled,
The pain that we must endure,
The times we travel forward,
The time for us to die.

In such a melancholy mandate
As we stand before ourselves,
A frozen understanding,
Our unwillingness to delve.

The directions we need to follow,
The inspirations of our fate,
The guile of indecision,
The road that we should take...

Keep the Faith

Is it too much to ask?
So much that I could have hoped for
Just a small white picket fence
In the serenity of our own backyard.

The simple comforts of a daily routine,
All so out of place as it now seems.
Once you were no longer around,
My dreams that could no longer be found.

It is so very much to want?
To simply have an adequate life?
Not necessarily a fairy tale,
But simply something that turned out all right.

Can it ever be the same?
Will I find a newer purpose for my life?
Can I transcend those memories?
I'll just have to try and keep the faith.

Old

On the rainy streets of existence,
The prior pathways lined with gold,
So much for your persistence
As you're continually growing old.

The former limelight in the darkness
When you once truly felt alive,
In a flash of youthful brightness,
Now you're just hoping to survive.

In such a melancholy mixture,
A slight glance against all of time,
Like a balloon just waiting to puncture
From the ruthless darts of the divine.

But there's a beauty of youth inside you,
Life's higher dreams about to unfold.
There's nothing that your spirit can't do
In getting those wings as you grow old.

Harder

I knew it wasn't going to be easy,
But it was so much harder than I'd imagined—
Seeing that thing would never be the same
After my life had turned into a wreck.

After the loss of what had seemed so normal,
Those little things we often take for granted,
As our families would gather for the holidays,
Those seeds of love we'd carefully planted.

Sometimes they chose to leave us
On that day that the romance was lost,
With just the hauntings of our former gatherings
As we come to grips with the ultimate cost.

Other times they had to depart us,
A loss of our love's incalculable cost,
As they were taken away for eternity
From the day their life was lost.

To feel alone and unknown,
Set apart from the living,
Just the mists of those memories
And the clouds of their misgiving.

The Water

It's so easy to falter
In this falsified life of ours.
With few chances of going higher,
So much for reaching for the stars...

In the myriad of our mixtures
Trying to find a hue that seems pure,
Against our pallet of presumptions,
Wanting to find something that's sure.

In a never-ending struggle
Like a search for our own special light,
Against this discouraging world
In hopes of finding what was always just right.

A little path across that stream bed,
The stepping stones you could never hope to alter,
In the quiet serenity of understanding
Like those perfect ripples upon the water.

118

Sunny Sundays

It all goes by so fast
And it will seem like an instant
When you look back years from now
Wishing it wasn't all so distant.

Daily responsibilities
When you feel like you've toiled in vain,
Taking care of family matters.
Someday, you'll wish for that again.

As they eventually grow up
And find their way out of the nest,
Giving you some peace and quiet
For such a greatly deserved rest.

But there were some sunny Sundays
And the quieter times at night
When that contentment was the treasure
And you knew that it was so very right.

Don't ever forget that
And value it while it lasts,
Because someday it will just be a memory,
A haunting ghost from your younger past.

Believer

By a certain whispering against the moonlight,
The special mysteries before the dawn,
From the depths of darkness to an insight,
Tomorrow is for carrying on.

In the short humanity of our dreams,
To live a life before it's taken away,
And just what that all really means
With every single passing day.

To choose to carry on forward
Or in fear remain chained to the back,
To embrace the onward and upward
Or suffer as your doubts are played back.

Simply giving yourself a new chance,
Never fearing the ultimate achiever,
So your life finally comes alive
As you become a new believer.

Tempest

In the throes of our experience,
With every single turn of the dice,
To pass on the streets of serenity,
Trying our toss against a futile night.

That look of the tears in her eyes,
The foreboding of troubled skies,
But with new hopes of true love,
That innermost fire never really dies...

Like a burning tempest in the twilight,
A supernatural glow underneath the moon,
With the emotions to fill an eternity,
Dreaming—*expecting*—the ecstasy soon.

The most human of all our drives,
In some ways, the very reason to live,
To hope that our fairy tale survives,
Trying against the fading light to stay alive…

Humanity

Sympathy,
Vanity,
Solidarity,
Inanity.

Realization,
Capitalization,
Isolation,
Reformation.

Standby,
Outcry,
Dignify,
Goodbye.

Humility,
Insanity,
Profanity,
It's all just a part
Of our own humanity.
　　　　　Think about it

SQUIT

SCARABAEAN

LACHRYMOGENIC

ACCOLADE

ANICULAR

MONADISM

TIPPET

DISCINCT

WONTLESS

PAVIS

MENISCUS

KYPHOSIS

MEDIUS

DRILL

DISTRIBUTIVE

DIFFRANGIBLE

HELIOTROPE

BORZOI

ROCHE

TRUE

PROOF
THE
PROVIDE
ACTIONS
YOUR
AND
TRUTH
OF THE
A LOVE
LOVE REQUIRES
TRUE
ROCHE
BORZOI
HELIOTROPE
DIFFRANGIBLE
DISTRIBUTIVE
DRILL

Smitten

Just as it was once written
In a different time and place
By the mechanics of humanity,
Those subtitle orbits in outer space.

From the gravitational fixtures,
The gentle pulls of those very waves,
In its sublime songs of density
Where the heaviest often saves.

For an inescapable horizon,
Like a burning star meant to explode,
The events beyond any short-term vision
Like a wanton vacuum ready to implode.

To just be put into our lonely boxes
By the four sides to keep them at bay.
With a bottom and top to constrain them,
The opaque are hidden from the light of day

But these are the things that must be opened:
To read those books that were previously written,
Breathing the light and the air all around them,
I'm afraid that I was just utterly smitten...

Reflections

There were reflections upon the water
Like the ripples across my life,
With those pictures of perseverance
Among the undercurrents of strife.

But also sunshine during the daylight
As the trees would flow with the breeze,
Among the warmest waters of happiness
When our feelings may do as they please.

Or the twinkling of a distant starlight
As they shine on the waters below,
When our Earth is reflecting their beauty
In a reverence it wants us to know.

Over the paths of least resistance,
Those waters will make their own way
Like the flows of our very existence
For the perfection of every day.

Serendipity among those sources
In their courses so well defined,
A natural mirror of our own loves
In our heart, soul, and mind.

The reflections upon those waters
Like the fluidity within our lives,
Among the eddies of endless currents
Where true honesty always survives...

Just

I just need a bit of attention
As a means to fill my end,
A little primal intervention
For a life I don't have to defend.

I just want a different cup,
A canvas on which I can paint,
And a mixer to mix things up
For new life beyond constraint.

I just need a brighter view,
Landscapes bent to my will.
The sunshine will always renew—
It's but a matter of careful skill.

I just want to have a chance
For a way to remain alive,
A memorable midnight dance,
What we all need to survive.

Evolution

To still be full of some life
In a mostly lifeless room,
To still have some sight of the hope
That it didn't die off so soon.

Perhaps it's a revolution
Or merely just a kink.
In my own evolution,
I'm not quite sure what to think.

Maybe a colder rendition
Of my old frozen ambition.
Through the warmth of my own breath,
All I can see is their own death.

Destroyed by their sovereignty,
The wonderful life they left behind,
Abandoning their humanity,
With no more chances for a rewind.

Not able to see the sunlight
Through the despair of their trees,
Just charcoaled remnants to remember
Where only the former innocent sees.

In a litany of lightning flashes
Across both the East and the West,
In disingenuous synapses
Because their minds were distressed.

The floods will surely come,
But then the rains will slowly go
Into the deadened drains
Of that person, they used to know.

Just the former sounds of thunder,
The record slowly spins around,
As they abandoned what they were,
No real sort of love will be found.

Clouds

Just another dark cloud, passing across my sky
In the fullness of my life as time passes by.

It may be that more will eventually come my way;
I choose to hope to look forward to a much better day.

Such is my life with some good mixed with the bad;
I want to see a better day that is happy rather than sad.

For our life is but a mix of so very many different things,
Children's happy voices and couples with wedding rings.

Memories of toil as well as perfect peace or turmoil,
Sunlit houses as we foster our plants in the garden soil.

So many things to consider and very important to us all,
Our parents who raised us and will eventually fall.

For some, this cloud can seem so very bleak and dark.
All the world against us seems so cold, bleak, and stark.

Struggling in all of this we will certainly find our way.
Through love, the sun will shine for a brighter new day.

Try

Do you know what will matter the most?
It's how you will live on after you die,
The changes you gracefully affected,
That perseverance that made you try.

And the stuff which will be remembered
Are the things which will always last,
Because you helped to forge a new future
From out of the ashes of your past.

And this present life will never stay,
But there is a hope that I want you to see.
As we cross the roadways of our lives,
We must help everyone to become free.

Expounding real wisdom in the light of day,
Being careful and considerate in what we say.
As humble people who express what we feel,
We must sparingly judge but readily heal.

There are many things we do while we're here
Out of our greed, envy, spite, and fear.
None of these will last past your very last day,
So please carefully consider these things that I say.

Memories of War

In battles for blood throughout the ages,
Fighting in a game of death that was real,
By the struggles and grief of a soldier's wages,
From their own last breaths for a true ideal.

The memories of war, still longing for life
In a forest of eyes as they lived by the gun,
On the forbidding seas like the edge of a knife,
For a nighttime of terror with each settling sun.

Mountains lead nowhere in the bitter cold,
Memories of the war that were fought on that day,
Despite the oppression, being brave and bold,
With a cost far greater for the price they'd pay.

Across the bleakness of the desert sands,
No place for any hope when confronting death.
Their very lives and liberty were in God's hands,
Storming the beaches before their last breath.

Memories of war while remembering their life,
Still hoping for a chance while facing their death,
To once again see their children and wife,
Remembering the past before that last breath.

In the sands of Europe on a deadly beach
Or in a jungle paradise that was true hell,
Among the frozen forests with all hope out of reach,
Our young men struggled as their brothers fell.

Memories of war, bloodshed, and dread,
Remembering the death and reliving the hate.
The history of books where the sadness was read
When the world was undone for a soldier's fate.

"Could I just have, please, just one more day…"
He was pleading as he took his very last breath—
"Dear God, please help me, help me find some way."
But in the history of war, it was just another death.

Misguided

Feeling used up,
Thrown away,
Hoping against hope
For a better day.

Feeling kind of old
As if all is lost.
Maybe it always was
At such a high cost.

Feeling complacent,
Not seeing where to go,
An unclear future,
Nothing left to know.

Feeling misguided,
Taking the wrong road,
Oppressively burdened
By that heavy load.

Feeling disenfranchised,
Misdirected ways,
But with connections cut,
The futility still stays.

Feeling kind of worthless
In a world before my sight.
If only value was given
To what was truly right.

Feeling a little deadened
By life, the knife has pared.
The losses were cut loose
But the serenity wasn't spared.

Feeling somewhat stupid,
As if I took a wrong turn,
Like a dead-end road
To a place that would burn...

Voices

As my constant companions,
Those little voices in my head,
Quiet yet demanding,
The things they said.

The only ones there:
Truth lighting my way,
Always ready to correct,
Knowing just what to say.

Their stories never change,
No swirling turbulence fought,
Consistent versus complacent,
The truth can't be bought.

Shifting human emotions
Are like the waves of the sea—
I know I can trust them,
Those little voices in me.

They're the only ones
Better off with me not dead,
Because of the fire within,
Those voices in my head.

No idle backstabbing,
Lying, treacherous deceit,
Adamant in understanding,
Never needing to retreat.

Not selfish or narcissistic,
Entrapments of fealty,
As if they could fool me,
Misjudging inner frailty.

Your only daily mantra,
A sorrowful underachiever,
Excuses in transparency
As a powerless deceiver.

They're constant companions,
But not quite Goldilocks
With an inner wisdom
As the voices talk....

Beyond...

We're all just travelers in outer space
On a lowly planet that we all call our home,
And I came to find myself in an unusual place,
Even though I always knew that we were never alone.

Tapped into unlimited inspiration
As the stars fluctuated in their luminous waves,
By their very essence of a new true creation,
That's simply the way that the universe behaves..

For they'll burn so ever brightly
But then eventually, they'll all die and fall
By their own "supernovalistic" tendencies
In the very dances that they do before us all.

Not so different from our own earthly life—
A bitter embroilment of forgiveness against envy.
In a battle to overcome our old weaknesses
Against our unwanted strife.

To exchange the insanity of our futile vanity.
For the freedom of a natural interpersonal unity,
Trying desperately to finally find a real true life...
Like an S.O.S from the farthest of any star

In a signal that demands you to respond
By a simple revelation of some truth from afar.
So you can launch your very own rocket...
Towards the brightest of any stars and far beyond...

Just a Candle

The silence across a lifetime,
The screams that were never heard,
An endless pit of mendacity,
The obvious was never observed.

Like a shadow upon the light switch,
Obscuring the off to on,
In such a dimly lit room light,
The contrast had long since gone.

In a powerless presentation,
Like a wick without a candle,
It's just the wax of human emotion,
Far more than you could handle.

In the presence of reality,
There are so few places we can hide.
It's better to be in the sunlight—
That's where you were meant to abide.

Fragility

The beauty of the heavens,
What it means to be just.
In this frailty of a world,
We absolutely must.

To understand existence,
Our place in outer space,
Overcoming the resistance,
Meeting it face to face.

Being better than you would be
In a battle that must be won,
Like the mists of utter darkness,
Overcome by the rising sun.

Realizing tranquility
When you set things aright,
No longer in futility
When you walk in the light.

No longer quite so aimless
As you feel the fabric of life.
The endless loops of music
That love rebirths from strife.

The myriad of second chances,
The traps of so many sins,
As our heart so entrances,
Humanity always wins.

But you must surpass this,
Become larger than yourself,
Like a book of great wisdom
Never destined for the shelf.

The remedy for fragility—
That's what we need to attain.
The answer for all humanity,
It's so hard for me to explain...

Force of One

Delirium in the anger,
A solace from all the pain.
Fingers point so carelessly,
Finding someone else to blame.

Like a marking after dark,
Unknowingly unseen,
In a human interaction,
Just as it's always been.

Offenses fraught with danger,
An equilibrium of one,
But the scales were out of balance,
As humanity was undone.

The egos pointed inward
While love should have pointed out,
Such a self-centered paradigm,
The birthplace of our doubt.

To see a higher meaning,
Trying to touch a greater place,
You will never ever get there
Unless you lift your eyes toward space.

Infinitesimal beings,
Specks of sand upon the beach,
Your life is electricity,
With those stars not hard to reach.

For power in persuasion
With the gift of being real,
By your willingness to suffer,
Facing all that you might feel.

Then to hit with a ball bat
When all has come undone,
Straightening the crooked,
You can be a force of one...

Hollowed Out

In the fog of ambiguity,
The daily grind of our lives,
Where only the strong recover
As determination survives.

The chances that we lost,
Those times we never kissed,
Far beyond any cost,
The memories that were missed.

The pulses of our heartbeats,
The resonance of our pain,
Containing the regrets
Of all that was lived in vain.

Like a hollowed-out container,
A vessel that was never filled,
There will be no remainder
As subtraction has finally willed.

Due Time

Our nature's stubborn cycles,
Repeating in spans of time,
Mystical views for the future,
As Gematria writes the divine.

With numbers all around us,
Dates cast among the stars,
On the highways underneath us
And some people in purple cars.

For what really is the future?
If it's all been seen from the past,
And what comes out of eternity,
If it was never intended to last.

For so it was written,
So, it will be done.
There's nothing new
Underneath the sun.

Obsessing over money,
Little figures on a screen.
In a world that's often lonely,
What did it really mean?

A chance to escape higher?
Leading from the divine?
As the mystery was known to me,
All in its due time...

Meanings

To take just a few simple words
And arrange them into a verse,
Then adding a little bit of wisdom
Which they can slowly try to disperse.

To shine a light towards the inner darkness
So that others are able to see
In the reflections of our minds—
That's what poetry means to me.

To live a life that's outside of regretting,
New meanings where you're totally free,
No longer avoiding by forgetting—
That's what poetry means to me.

To follow the heart's inner leanings
Like a lock in search of a key,
And then eventually understanding—
That's what poetry means to me...

Falling Star

Trying to catch a falling star
Or ride a losing wave,
The knives seemed less sharpened
Like there was something left to save.

The star that burned the brightest
Would be the first one to fall,
But I'm still yearning and burning,
Always trying to stand tall.

Regardless of the faults,
My many mistaken ways,
Paths of utter confusion,
Across the delusive days.

The chances not realized,
A game that was never won,
Not quite materialized,
Just the waste of what's undone.

Memories as a vapor,
Futility at its best,
A past that couldn't last
For a life that failed the test.

But it wasn't going to be me
Although I used to burn so bright.
Because I heard the stars from afar,
I gained a different insight.

About being truthful,
Totally transparent,
So my life wasn't futile,
It became so apparent...

For better or for worse,
Placing good against the bad,
It's a level that you realize
From the experience that you've had.

Folded Wings

So high up in the sky,
The place we ought to be.
It's not so hard if you try
When you realize...

What it is to be free.

Understanding grace,
Wisdom as a power,
Like the stars from out of space
Send their own meteor shower.

The sun glints on the horizon
As our world warms to receive it.
Iridescently explosive,
If only you chose to believe it...

Cycles of existence,
Heartbeats along the way.
Overcome the resistance!
Let your powers come out to play.

Take the folded wings we're hiding,
Let them live to see the day,
Unbound by our fearfulness,
Those things we're scared to say.

Those things so hard to do!
Like our life was just a mistake,
So unsure of our bearings,
Just how much we can take...

But please listen to me,
I'm no stranger at trying to survive,
And I've sensed through my survival
What it means to be alive.

Never pass any of it by,
Things you were scared to try.
There's no life in any lie,
But the truth will always try...

Ready

Falling emotions,
Failing breath,
Faded devotions,
Finally death.

Rising regrets,
Rebounding all,
Remembering before,
Ready to fall.

Falling patience,
Failing needs,
Faded relations,
Finally freed.

Rising awareness,
Rebounding mind,
Remembering myself,
Ready to refine.

Falling places,
Failing the fee,
Faded agitations,
Finally, I see.

Rising division,
Rebounding strife,
Remembering serenity,
Ready for new life.

Falling out of sight,
Failing the test,
Faded regurgitation,
Finally, I know best.

Rising peace,
Rebounding drive,
Remembering again,
Ready to be alive.

Scared

Life had been good in many ways,
Yet bitterness still found its place.
All the years lost in yearnings,
They were written on his face.

Is this all that there is?
To be put away on a shelf?
A forgotten book of sorrows,
Left to rot by itself.

He couldn't help but wonder
Why must we suffer this strife,
Remembering the past,
That day he lost his wife.

The struggles of his work,
What he'd hoped to attain.
It was all just insanity,
Only to end in such pain.

His glimmering children
When they came into his world,
His daughters twinkling eyes
As old memories whirled.

His son's accomplishments
To become so very great,
But have to leave so early
Through a tragedy of fate.

No longer having a home,
No faces he really knew,
Being so cold and alone
With nothing left to do.

It took so long to get there,
The ups and downs of his ride.
It would all end soon enough
While he lived the downhill slide.

Then he'd be just a memory,
No longer having to be scared,
But he wouldn't be remembered
Because no one really cared.

Straight to Your Heart

Straight to your heart,
You can feel life's pain—
A world of emptiness,
Something ventured…

Nothing gained.

Straight to your heart
As it rips you in two—
Trying to hold it together
Since that's all you can do.

Straight to your heart,
Just you, all alone—
A prison of regrets,
Happiness unknown.

Straight to your heart,
Every crooked mile—
Upside down pathways,
Forcing every smile.

The Light She Was Meant to Find

In a trembling life,
Weary but not broken,
So much left unsaid,
Never to be spoken.

Paths that weren't sure,
The daybreak not clear.
In the last of the past,
The only thing left was fear.

But a dream far beyond
The chance to make life right,
Like a sunrise over the sea
With its endless rays of light.

Perhaps by sheer will
And the focus of her mind,
She'll see it right before her:
The light she was meant to find.

Intense

We were meant to be intense;
That's the way I see it.
Transcending pretense
To find our perfect fit.

The most seductive smile,
The greatest feeling gained,
That touch of taste and style,
For a love unrestrained.

Delirium of the delirious
For a love so oblivious,
Like an unending fire
With the heat to inspire.

The gift of omnipresence
Against a tumult of tears,
To cut our very essence,
Abandon all our fears.

And through life's darkness
There comes a glimmer of light,
A flash of hopefulness,
A chance to make it right.

Only from our own tears
We reach toward the light;
From our darkest fears
We want to make things right.

Signals

Dancing through the galaxy,
Starbursts across her hair.
An ethereal Milky Way,
Swirling without care.

And I was calling for her
Into the depths of space.
My words were the beacon
For her much-needed grace.

Signals plain as I could make them,
A heart's a simple distress call,
Pleading from humanity,
Before my lonely fall.

Louder and stronger
As clear as a bell,
Simple and pure,
Only time would tell.

But poetry has a power—
Words rewire the brain.
I'm an expert technician,
My words aren't in vain.

As I gain an understanding
From darkness to light,
I'll wire it all carefully,
Those words will make it right.

Just a Few Memories

Just a few memories
Like slowly sifting sand,
The harder crystal facets
Weren't as soft as I once planned.

Failing ever gently,
Falling slowly as they flow,
Over endless sands of life
To their places down below.

Towards a clear sea of glass
As every hour sifts away,
Congealing your own life,
Becoming clear as the day.

Never being filled again
Or turned upside down,
With no way of reliving it,
Only being left to drown.

The hourglass always measures
The remaining time that it takes,
The occasional sparkling crystals,
The overspill of mistakes.

Relentlessly all draining
Until regrettably gone,
Just fragile pieces of glass
Remembering all along.

In beautiful containers,
Clarity always rebuts,
For rare gems in the sand
Or a life's sharpest cuts.

Life

To be alive
Or not to be,
That's the question
In front of me.

To be able to survive,
Perhaps live free,
Like a dark dilemma
I regretfully see.

To make some way
By a past unbound,
A whole new day,
Can freedom be found?

Life is just a blink
Against an all-seeing eye,
Not always as we think
Before the day we die.

It's what we paint on the canvas,
Mixing colors with our knife.
Truth those hues encompass
This *is* our very *life*.

We're all on display
In a gallery of the mind.
Souls, we can't betray
As we hope to be refined.

What could I ever say
To make you understand?
You must carefully choose your way
To remain within God's hand.

You may not think this matters
As your vigor slowly fades away,
But someday when that life shatters,
You'll painfully wish for this day.

Colors

I was looking at the windows
Within a million rays of light,
The intricacy of their colors
As if everything was all right.

Reflecting off the walls,
The refractions tell a story,
A stained-glass expression
In all its ethereal glory.

About the tainting of our pasts,
The tints that life seems to give,
A delicate balance of artwork,
Easily broken while we live.

A picture that's so transparent,
Leaded pieces fit to the mold,
Being cut within our places
To fade away as we grow old.

Forevers
after Emily Dickinson

"Forever – is composed of Nows –"
The lives you lead every day,
The other forevers you touch,
Eternities within each day.

Seas of human tranquility,
The battles against the storms.
It's by your embracing of civility
A more beautiful sunset forms.

With a measure of temperance
By understanding our conditions,
The flux of our human existence
And its self-centered inhibitions.

To live is to take that chance,
Even if you don't know how,
That you can make the world better
Because your forever starts now...

Emily Dickinson once said, " Forever is comprised of nows –"
I think she was on to something there.

Big Stuff

Life's full of really big questions.
Why do our loved ones have to die?
The myriad of reflections
When we're forced to say goodbye.

The stars so far above our grasp,
The seas below our reach.
Is it too much to ask,
What this life of ours will teach?

The great mysteries of science,
All of the particles spinning around
In such a dynamic alliance
By which everything is bound.

Creatures both great and small,
The way we all became alive,
Never far from our own nature's call
In the lowest struggles to survive.

There are so many beautiful flowers
Yet a world awash in hate,
Battling among the powers
Against our own human fate.

It's all the really big stuff—
Whoever, whatever, whenever,
As if we could consider enough
The questions that last forever.

Through the Door

By currents of our lives,
The stars within our dreams,
It's not so far be fetched
Being easier than it seems.

Coagulating emotions,
Touching those things within,
In the dance across our lives
To a place we've never been.

Extraordinary awareness
With a finger on the dial,
Finely tuned the resonance
In your own house of style.

A vibrancy of colors,
An orchestra of light.
You are your own conductor;
It's time to play things right.

Like a song of deep remembrance
Giving power to see beyond,
Going ever so slowly upward,
Willing time for you to respond.

To scream at the single universe
Because it chose to place you here,
But you are a part of eternity
And you have no more reason to fear.

Only the grand opportunity
To become what is fitting and right,
Casting past the forgotten darkness
To then become alive in the light.

As a beacon of the simple truths,
An example of selfless love,
Just being a humble little person
Under those great stars above.

A life had been given to you
With only one time around,
So shine like those sparkling stars—
Let your true love abound.

PART FOUR:
love, lust, and loss

Let You Go

How high that we could see
For a life in the stars above,
How good to feel so free,
How right to be so much in love.

It was so very fitting,
The fact that we'd even met,
For a new chance at living
Far past our old regrets.

So we could feel alive then,
The perfect balance of a new romance,
Going someplace we've never been to
In such a victorious circumstance.

But the tears on my face
Had to let it slip away.
There was nothing I could say or do
So I had to let you go.

All the things you showed me,
All the love that we once lived,
While all that time you'd saved me,
Then I had to let you go.

Not just forever
But forever and a day.
You were the love of my life
And that memory will always stay...

The beautiful choice that we made,
Till death do we part,
And although you slipped away from me,
You'll always live inside my heart.

Questions

She asks things I like to answer,
She says things I want to hear.
Although she's far away from me,
Somehow, she feels very near.

Regardless of all the places,
Times that we had once talked,
It was as if it was all in a forest
On paths that we had once walked.

Reflections on the simpler things,
An understanding that was true,
Verbally painting new pictures,
Something I really liked to do.

Enhanced by the enchantment.
Because of our newfound base,
Two talkers in a world of silence,
Talking openly face-to-face.

Whatever limits to what we could say,
Restraints against what we might do,
In a world of hidden sentiments,
It was overcome by just us two

Make Some Waves

The waves of the sea were calling to me
In a gentle, rhythmic way,
A turquoise ocean's song of love
As I walked along the beach today.

With sparkling sands beneath my feet,
New serenity for my mind,
Hoping for someone that I would meet,
The brightest light that I could find.

The waves of the sea were calling for me
As the sun warmed us from above.
On that beach, it seemed within reach—
I could find my one true love.

New expressions of a world for me,
A place I would want to call home.
Vast expanses where I could run free,
No longer ever being alone...

No Flowers

No walk in the park,
No relationship bliss,
No games after dark,
Only all that's amiss.

No time on the beach,
No promising day,
It's so far out of reach,
There's nothing left to say.

No reason to eat out,
No excuse to leave home,
Just the silence of doubt
When you're there all alone.

No flowers to buy,
No candy today,
No sweetness was left,
For this Valentine's Day...

Feel Again

I just couldn't help but see her,
That electric glow on her hair,
Lights vibrantly modulating
With laser beams filling the air.

I just couldn't help but think about
How something here felt surreal,
Like a climax far past its brink
For a love that was finally real.

All the dance floor was spinning
As the pairings united by grace,
In our own ethereal galaxy,
In our own very personal place.

As if nothing else really mattered,
No sorrow or regrets from our will,
The cages of loneliness shattered,
Our hearts never standing still.

And no longer remaining silent
As they screamed to the heavens above,
Because love is the foundation of life
And life is the very essence of love.

And those feelings are deep vibrations
To resonate with your very soul,
Our hearts chase those variations
Until they're finally remade whole.

In needing a powerful spark
To alight their most hidden meanings,
Lives walking out of the dark,
To follow the heart's secret leanings.

Sometimes finding a treasure,
Sometimes just crying in vain,
But in their courage to hopelessly venture,
That they might finally feel again.

The One

He saw a sparkle in her eyes
Against the dance floors glow,
Swirling motions of starlight
As his time began to slow.

And with every little flicker,
The many sounds all around,
Melting into emotions,
As if love was finally found.

Around and around,
Forever divine,
Twirling through his heart,
Dancing through his mind.

Expectations,
Palpitations,
Perspirations,
Reverberations.

Then again and again
With every new drop,
The chance of a lifetime
For a dance that won't stop.

In the most perfect harmony
To meet the rising sun,
He just knew in his heart
That she had to be the one.

Fallen

I think I was ultimately captured
In an instant, at the speed of light,
Against the might of my resistance
Because it seemed so utterly right.

I suppose I was simply a victim
Of the sparks that you had to show,
To blast past my deliverance,
As if you were the only one—
                     I wanted to know

I guess there was just no chance for me
In our hopeless stories of love,
As I suddenly saw the opportunity
When your burning light
                 came down from above.

I'm afraid that I've simply fallen
For the subtle enchantments in your face,
Like the very stars were calling for me
Towards the hidden galaxies
                   of your beautiful grace.

The End

Neither hugs nor kisses
Or just hints of some love,
Not even near misses
Before push became shove.

Neither talking sincerely
To relate something true,
But suffering severely
Before my own coup.

Neither life ever lightened
With enlightened remarks,
But a noose that was tightened
By those fireless sparks.

Neither smiling nor solace
To quench all the pain,
In a life that was awe-less
Under skies filled with rain.

Neither oneness nor comfort
To help right every wrong,
But the vacuum of loss,
Deadened space all along.

Neither secrets so special
Or anything dear,
It was just superficial
For the ending was near…

The end.

Supercharger

From the cold of a long-fought winter,
The oppression of its overcast skies,
There came a fire that was soon to follow
That sudden spark in the gleam of her eyes.

As a tempest in the midst of my turmoil
With an energy that I couldn't compare,
To lay the tracks of love before me,
For a race far beyond any dare.

Like the twinkling of a distant starlight,
She would warm my frozen heart,
By her powerful forces of love,
To give me a way to finally restart.

And just like a supercharger,
She revved the engine of my soul,
Flywheels were spinning wildly,
Their revolutions out of control.

Then just like a rocket,
She shot me to the moon!
So far up there in the air,
I wouldn't be down anytime soon.

But just like a volcano,
She melts me where I stand,
But I really don't mind the heat
Though it's a little out of hand.

And just like a river,
She carried me along
With her many endless currents.
My God, they were strong!

But just like a mountain,
She placed me on the peak,
And the ice was even nice,
I felt so very weak.

Then just like a forest,
She held me by her trees,
Their leaves gently swaying,
Mesmerized in her breeze.

And just like an oasis,
She blessed a barren land.
Past my dunes of wanton strife,
I could see diamonds in her sand.

But just like the moonlight,
She gave closure to my days,
By the serenity of her beauty
In the captivation of her gaze.

And then just like a meadow,
She was painting for the sun.
With some flowers for my mind.
She was definitely the one...

Other Worlds

In an electromagnetic blaze,
Like a halo encircles the sun,
A tempest of fiery temptation,
I could tell that she was the one.

The keys to a strong addiction,
In the way that it's satisfied,
Lightning dissolving the twilight,
When my heart had fully complied.

Somehow, I knew it was right,
Certain wisdom was granted to me,
Seeing newly as never before
As I prepared to be set free.

Like opening a greater door,
Anticipating what's beyond,
Other worlds were waiting for me
With no choice but to simply respond.

By the uttermost simple harmony
And a voice I could almost hear,
In the very softest of melodies
As her power drew ever near.

In the starlit rifts of the galaxy
From the mysteries of its deepest space,
The many wonders that I could see
And I could see it all within her face.

For a whole new understanding
With no need for complexity,
Ever demanding and commanding
By their galactic synchronicity.

And for keeping my soul alive
As it was suddenly revived,
Towards that ever-increasing light
Because she was so wonderfully bright.

Burnt Pathways

In the black forest of my memory,
There were bleak paths of despair,
Forgotten by the glowing embers,
Burnt landscapes in need of repair.

I tried to climb the mountains,
Wanting desperately to see,
But the smoke stung my eyes
Because I still wasn't free.

Then waiting by the meadows
As if the flowers were still alive,
But sunlight doesn't come easy
Though the ashes always survive.

I was waiting for you,
But the fires never came.
You never returned—
The ashes were to blame.

Love

When you love so much that it hurts,
You understand what it is to live,
Then your soul begins to testify
Of just who it is and meant to give.

This is the way we're designed
With this unique traumatic force,
As you seek the higher ground
To find your one and only source.

The visions that always haunt you
As machinations of your mind.
Life's barriers that will daunt you
When you seek what you need to find.

Your heart cries by hope slowly dying
But never lose sight of your way,
Press on toward new fulfillment
And let that love burn brightly today.

Ecophobia dynamite Lumpenintelligen Flummery memories help regret paranoia loss reverence humor robots solitude Deorsumversion dialoge rhyme Pantomnesia werewolf Inspissate Accinge variations stories lust whereout

Mismatch

A world just a little out of sync,
Like a record needle off its track,
A strobe light's dimming blink
Or an amp with no input jack!

Will the tubes ever glow again?
Can the circuits be re-powered
With wavelengths for the brain
Or have the sources all been soured?

But the cats were still cavorting
As the Bluetooth headphones flashed,
Making this life a bit less contorted
Through the songs that the DJ mashed.

But the tractors would still traverse
And those chickens will always scratch,
Stuck in a box with the adverse
In a totally failed mismatch...

Emptiness

The songbird flew down and asked me,
"What is it like to truly love?"
I no longer had any answer,
So, I asked, "What's it like to fly so far above?"

Then an old apple tree inquired,
"What does it mean to have a fruitful life?"
I didn't know what to say, except,
"Have you ever been carved by a dull knife?"

And then the large rock wanted to know,
"Do you ever worry when the winds blow?"
Perplexed, all that I could think of was,
"Are you always so steady within that flow?"

Lastly, the clouds wondered wistfully,
"Have you ever wanted to see into our sky?"
But my only truthful answer was,
"Only when the oceans of life became dry..."

Crushing

It was just a crush
The walls couldn't hide,
An emotional rush,
A desperate ride.

Blinded by the light,
What could I say?
So very bright
Though there was no way.

Nothing cast in stone
In my darkened room,
Forever alone,
Ending too soon.

Eventually crushing
As it grinds to a halt,
No longer rushing
An emotional fault.

A Garden

If I could build a garden,
A garden especially for you,
I would plant it all carefully
In a glowing natural way, too.

Flowing shapes as a living creature,
Having parts both new and old,
A diversity of varied species,
Blooming in both warm and cold.

The complementary coexistence
Would not be so easy to make,
But so beautiful once completed,
Coming alive and becoming awake.

If I were to build that garden,
I would want you to help me too.
If I were to build that garden,
I would want to build it for you.

Bang, Bang, Bang

Bang, bang, bang!
Like a shot in the head,
I was brought back alive
To finally live instead.

Bang, bang, bang!
With a bullet to the heart
By the guns of love
From the very start.

Slash, slash, slash!
Cut my heart in two
Like a razor blade
That was held by you.

Smack, smack, smack!
Hit me with a board;
Your crippling beauty
Is what I adored.

Crash, crash, crash!
Bring my glass house down
With the hardest rocks
That you've ever found.

Sting, sting, sting!
By your endless fire,
To be burned alive
Is what I desire.

Nip, nip, nip!
Cut me down to size
With your softest voice
And the light in your eyes.

Slide, slide, slide!
Toss me on my head,
You're breaking my balance
By the things that you said.

Thump, thump, thump!
Pound me into the ground
With your driving force
When you always astound.

Crash, crash, crash…
But I'll never burn,
I'm just waiting for you
Because it's your turn…

170

Sonnet 18 2.0
after William Shakespeare

Should I compare you to a summer's day?
Could I ever hope to find just the right way?
For you're lovelier than any sun's shine,
Both temperate and gentle within your time.

Rough winds shake the budding life of May,
Soon summer gives warmth in its short day,
But sometimes the heat overwhelms that place.
Nature's beauty may dim, but never your face.

The fairest forms of life so often decline
By untrimmed chance, or nature's course.
Your eternal beauty is a treasure of mine,
The unfading summers of your life's clear force.

Through your breeze of gentle wavering
Because your soft warmth will never fade,
Not losing possession of life's favoring,
Death never destroys what was made.

Could I ever hope to find a true and fitting way?
I don't think that I can ever hope that I could.
There's is so much more I would have to say
Because you're brighter than the fairest day…

Write It Off

I had to write it all off
In the books of the heart,
Erasing vibrations
So my waves could restart.

I had to pass it all by,
The things I would think,
Just the haunting of ghosts
Like invisible ink.

I had to clear the bookshelves,
Discard them by stages,
Ripping off bindings
From the unwritten pages.

I had to silence the stories
That would never exist,
In the dead of night,
Disappeared in the mist…

Starfall

As the moon broke the horizon
To reach for the twilight sky,
Rising past my wishful grasps.
If only I could fly…

In the coldness of that night,
A beauty still abounds
With the softest hints of starlight,
But it didn't mean love would be found.

A coldness in your voice,
The alienation of your eyes,
Leaving me without any choice,
My enemy in disguise.

As your heart grew silent,
Waves crashed against the shore.
On the dull sands of indifference,
There would be nothing more…

The deceitfulness of magic—
It's all just sleight of hand,
Wistfully wishing for harmony
Until truth played the final hand.

Breathe it in now,
Hear me as I'm calling,
While it turns upside down
Being faithful to your falling.

Completely out of balance
With voices of confusion,
In dispassionate violence,
It was all just an illusion.

Breathe it in now,
Be faithful to your calling,
While the world grows dark,
As your stars are quickly falling.

In and out

It was kind of hazy
Like a cloud around my mind,
A feeling beyond perception,
I just wondered what I'd find.

In and out.
In and out of my head
By a heart's ambitions,
The lonely books to be read.

Up and down,
Swirling around,
Calling out to me,
Just wanting to be found.

The very base of emotion,
The simple things that she said,
But twirling so violently,
I just couldn't get her out of my head...

Wishing Upon a Star

She's like a night full of lightning,
Gasoline thrown on a fire,
In a combustion of explosions
Far above my embers of desire.

Ominous eyes in the forest,
Glowing as if I should fear,
But she overwhelmed my apprehension
And I just wanted her to come near.

As if she was from a different time
To meet me in a brand-new place,
An intersection with the divine,
That beautiful look on her face…

And the sheer majesty of her thoughts,
The many things I sensed within,
Like someone made just for me,
Disregarding the consequence of sin.

I saw inside her doubtful mind—
It was like
Exploding stars in the galaxy.
I hoped she would understand
That she needed to be set free…

To take her proper place
Within the depths of creativity,
Like the queen of outer space!
Those things that live eternally.

Sometimes,

The star that burns the brightest
Is the first one that falls,
Not seeing the love before them
From the blindness of those walls.

In the eternity of her essence…
Overwhelming omnipresence.
Could I ever hope to wish upon a star?
So very close,
                Yet so very far…

Magic

I just couldn't quite explain it—
The power she seemed to have over me,
As if there was a dream within my touch
For a story of what life should be.

But I couldn't quite redeem it,
The very freedom of that lofty prize,
And all I could do was dream it
By that dreamy sparkle within her eyes.

And I could really see it,
That she could take me to a different place,
Past the stars of my present galaxy
For a ride far beyond outer space.

I could feel it with every sensation
As they called for me to break free,
For a hopeful ride beyond my life
Because she was utterly magical to me...

Beautiful in Blue

What gives life to a sensation?
What words would it have to say?
About life and the reasons for living
As a deeper spirit comes into play.

What does it really mean to be in love?
Is it just another form of infatuation?
Or is it being amazed as you gaze into the waters,
Enthralled by the clarity of their reflections…

What makes for the perfect entanglement?
The gravity of a star holding the orbit of your earth,
A power that separates the dead from the living
With the musical rhythms of a new rebirth.

What a pure and simple feeling it can bring
That stretches past the mysteries of time
As you touch those stars far beyond you
Towards the inward complexities of the divine.

She was so beautiful in blue
With a passion that burned the deepest red.
By her effortless motions of emotions,
I wouldn't be able to get her out of my head.

But she was also quite beautiful in white
Like the pristine snows of a winter's fairy tale.
Somehow, everything felt just right.
I wondered if our ship was going to set sail…

And she was very beautiful in green
Like an emerald sparkling in the forest.
I pondered—is this what love means?
Because I was starting to feel it in earnest.

She was so brightly beautiful in yellow
Like a field of flowers with sunshine above.
So softly sweet and mellow,
But maybe it wasn't about the colors…

I think I was just falling in love…

Forever True

I could see her in the sunlight,
I could sense her by the waves,
I could feel her with the moonlight.
That's simply how love behaves.

I could tell when she was singing
Along with the soft summer breeze,
In the most natural harmony
Where love could do as it pleased.

I could wish it would last forever
Or even forever and a day,
Because I believed in the mystery
That true love will make a way.

I could tell it was something special,
Extraordinarily right,
Erasing the twilight of a lifetime
To be replaced by her hopeful light.

Disappear From You

Extraordinarily beautiful,
The very incarnation of our lives,
In the delirium of so many senses
Where the inner spirit always survives.

To bring us on past the turmoil,
The purpose that a new chance creates,
For the makings of a fresh reality,
Running away from our previous fates.

The slightest wisps long forgotten
Of hope in the old dreams of love,
Songs of life that were abandoned
When push would then come to shove.

Like a faded, invisible memory
In a life that could never last,
The evaporations of eternity
For yet another ghost of the past.

In the perfect balance of nothing,
The very absence of the color black,
I'll suddenly disappear from you
And I'll never be coming back...

Come to Me

With a certain trembling presence
By just the slightest lilt in her voice,
It cut into my soul's very essence
Like an unforgivable angel of choice.

Past the myriad of all my memories,
A wonderment against the old pains,
Recalling the potential harmonies,
Weighing those losses against the gains...

In the merry-go-rounds of our mischief,
Like a carnival where you can't ever win,
To shoot in vain at unreachable targets,
Games of chance in the temperance of sin.

Where you're forced to then somehow try it
Against the odds of an unwinnable game,
Just trying until you're almost dying
While in the meantime you go insane...

In the reverberations across a lifetime,
Those echoes that go around in your head,
There's always a little hope for some sunshine,
The possibilities of what's been left unsaid.

In the vacuum of a wanton loneliness,
The very starkness I don't want to see,
There can be solace in our togetherness.
I simply need you to come to me...

Against the ether of a forlorn darkness,
The situations displaced in vain,
But love is not that far past kindling
And that mystery can be had once again.

For the dynamic of a newfound interlude,
For a way past those former pains,
Lest we die in our own inner solitude...
And pass the chance we have to live again.

Twirling

It's as if with a sword that I do fight,
Twirling words to make things right,
Dance music with its rhythm divine,
Flowing the phrases in perfect time.

For it's me, and I am like no other,
Searching for a match to improve one another,
And as the planets spin, so do I
Like I can extend my finger and touch the sky.

My mind is like that when I light it up,
As I see the depths in a clear glass cup. I can see…
What will I do and what might I find?
I laugh, twirl, and cry in my mind. As I laugh…

As I make my way through the galaxy,
Past the stars with the brightest glows,
She hides somewhere in the Milky Way
And she's the only star that knows.

Is she out there and does she care?
When I find shall I ask her and do I dare?
What shall I do, for I'm a complex one?
I need all my shadows to be filled by the sun.

This insight needs to finally sight me in
So I can go to a place that I've never been.
For a spark in the dark that will jolt me to run,
Then I want to have her when the day is done.

Supersonic

Like some lightning after midnight
To jolt the darkest want from my skies,
A whirlwind that utterly tumbled me
From the fire that burned in your eyes.

As if the universe was underneath me
With stars spiraling around our grace,
In the tumult of those glowing emotions
And the all-knowing smile across your face.

And I was utterly out of balance,
Trying my best to just get a grip!
But you completely overwhelmed me
With the perfect curves of your perfect lips.

I was on a whole different level now;
You'd taken me to a brand-new place,
Because your beauty was supersonic!
Blasting me off into outer space...

And you were like a great explosion,
Like the wildest of all carnival rides!
A wine glass that would never run empty
When I tried you out for size.

To touch the heat of those wanton stars
On our own heavenly playground,
As you came into an orbit so near
Where we went around and around and around...

Endless Summer

It was so classic!
And utterly fantastic!
When I first saw you on the beach,
Thinking you were out of my reach.

But I just had to try before I die.
You overwhelmed my doubt and fear,
That heavenly glow in your eyes.
I just had to bring you near...

With the stars in the sky
And the moon on your hair,
To abandon our old care
For a romantic solar flare.

Come to me, baby,
And don't you be shy.
With the whole summer before us
Let's just give it a try
                    And see....

Then, when I pulled you near
And kissed your lips for the first time.
It was electricity in action
For a little taste of the divine.

And the sparks couldn't tear us apart
As the waves crashed upon the shore
In their melodious synchrony
With a whole lot more in store...

With the universe spinning around us
And the warm sand beneath our feet,
I knew that you were that one in a million,
The special lady that I was supposed to meet

But when our summer had come to an end,
There wasn't any more reason to pretend.
The real heat of that season was within us
And there was no reason that it had to end.

Now I know that there's an endless summer
Where we can always run free,
Swirling in the warmth of our own sunshine
That new love
        Just between you and me…

ecstasy   imagination   cats

      werewolf   variations   stories

      roller skates   rhyme   comfort

solitude   thoughtfulness   lu

      reverence   humor   robots

regret   paranoia   loss

    humility   memories   help

awe   dynamite   supercharger

Too Long

A little too lonely
For a little bit long,
Trapped in the melancholy,
The greyer shades of life's song.

A little too silent
As if something's amiss,
In lacking the basics
Of even a simple kiss.

No laughter or harmony
In a close or personal way,
Just a dark ambiguity
With no one to hear or say.

No sunny walks in the park,
Just the vacuum of the dark,
Where life becomes stark
Because no love plays a part.

Love is Love

There's no need to try and change it,
The essence of our hearts and minds,
Or to ever rearrange it,
Those little things that a heart finds.

Regardless of the pain
Or a sunny day on the beach,
What you thought that you'd gain
But was somehow out of reach.

In the undying ebb and flow
With every one of your heartbeats,
Trying so hard to take it slow,
Apprehensive of your own defeat.

In the bravery to take a chance,
Driven by your innermost fires,
Emotion's pheromone dance
As our base humanity requires.

For every single heart that desires,
There's a place in their special sun,
Regardless of what transpires
There's still that most special one…

Searching through the forlorn wreckage,
Those mistakes made across our lives,
Trying to find something real to salvage
Where the remnant of a love survives.

Trying desperately to make it stay
Or for the rebound after the fall.
Somehow it all makes a way
For love is love, after all…

Facing It

I can still see the sparkle on your hair
And remember that special place
In the eye of my mind's lost love,
That night we went to outer space…

In the trials of a lonely dance floor,
Our willingness to try and transcend,
To hope there would be more in store,
But even the most perfect of stories
                sometimes come to an end

The letter had been carefully signed,
As if for a means of my affliction,
That love I'd had on my mind
To revisit my old addiction…

Your words, so tasteless and dry,
In such a practical sort of way,
There was no more reason to try
Unappetizing emotions that day.

Yet I refrained,
because my love remained,
Since the screams inside
Left me no place to hide…

Because what you often need
Are in the things that you know,
By the hopefulness of your dreams
Where the gardens of love can grow.

But we were hiding from the lightning,
By the very powers of life and death,
Under the stars of our fiery illusions,
Counting on love with a bated breath.

The rain chased our deepest fantasies
For a storm that would quench the fires,
As the embers in your eyes grew silent
For a change of heart in a soul's desires…

So at least we got to know each other,
Like asters grace the fields by their glow,
The warmest parts of beauty I'd admired
Before autumn covered the fields below.

The flowers in my mind became a memory
As coldness gripped the stars in space,
In a wintery loss of my hopeless love,
But damn,
        I could still see your face…

Haunting me day and night,
True love was in my sight.
I thought everything was all right,
But now,
        It's back to an endless twilight.

Where the seasons no longer accomplish
The joy that they used to bring,
With those flowers all dead and dying,
Where the birds refused to sing…

If...

If I were married to someone like her,
I would write her a thousand poems
Of life and love in worlds of wonder,
Of lights illuminating unknowns.

I would listen carefully to what she said,
Immersed with a bated breath.
I would feel her sunshine across my skies,
Fiercely love her until my own death.

If I were married to someone like her,
The world would be a different place.
I would see the light within her eyes,
The gracefulness upon her face.

Realize in the love of what I had,
Like a dream that was fully alive,
Having a reason to live in this world
And wanting it all to survive.

If I were married to someone like her,
I'd explore the whole galaxy,
Feeling the stars of her inner mind
As they're powerfully running free,

The universe where she quietly lives
By the rising of a distant moon,
Sunrise on so many different worlds
Where each day ended all too soon.

If I were married to someone like her,
My past would be all undone,
Regrets of life and the chances lost,
Those battles now finally won...

Girl

What does the sun have in common
With the rising of every new moon?
Why do those birds sing their songs
As if we've understood them all along…?

Why are all the planets in motion?
What does the universe have to teach?
I think it's a story of perpetual devotion
As sure as the serenity of a calming beach.

Why are all the flowers so beautiful
With the many colors they have to show?
The very wiles of their psychedelic smiles,
I think it just depends on who you know.

Why is there always that certain someone
That you would never want to live without?
The freshest breeze, caressing the trees,
Leaving your own forest without any doubts.

Why does life seem so much like a record?
The enchanting melodies spinning around.
Girl, I hope that I know you forever,
Playing the most beautiful music that I've found.

Walking in a Dream

I saw that little smirk on your face
With just the slightest hint of a smile
While I walked by quite indifferently
Although I'd been watching you all the while.

Like I was just walking in a dream,
Wondering if your hints were like they seemed.
So I asked if you wanted to come out and play,
The best thing that's happened to me today…

Reeling from the feelings,
Pheromones burning my brain,
Questioning myself,
Will I be able to see you again?

Taking a little chance for a dance,
I just know you'll fit like a glove.
But in the meantime, I'm quite intrigued,
Maybe it's even love…

Yes, I was walking in a dream
And you're the object of my desire.
In a hopeless entanglement of will
I'll do whatever you may require…

The lights are on, and the stage is set,
An intimate dance that I'll never regret,
To make the most of my bouncing bet
For a night I don't think I'll ever forget…
                        With the best yet to come…

Burn Me

You burn me
Then you chill…
Always misleading me
Against my own will.

You push me
Then you pull me
Always deceiving me
As I play the fool…

You quiet me
But then you scream,
A life of delusion
Like I'm in a bad dream.

You want me
And then you reject,
Unwinnable battles
In a life of regret.

CENTO
ROCHE
BORZOI
HELIOTROPE
DIFFRANGIBLE
DISTRIBUTIVE
DRILL
MEDIUS
KYPHOSIS
MENISCUS
PAVIS
WONTLESS
DISCINCT
TIPPET
MONADISM
ANICULAR

Shake Me

Love shook my heart
Like the wind through the trees,
Rumblings of the mountains,
The tumult of the seas.

Love carried me away
Like endless ocean waves,
A chance of happenstance
Deciding who it saves.

Love enlightened me
Being so far from death,
Like morning's first dew
As an entirely new breath.

Love took my heart,
Breaking life's chains,
The prisons of my past—
None of that remains.

PATHIC
ALIENILOQUY
PEREGRINATION
HAEMAIC
SULCALIZE
PANTOMNESIA
MILEOMETER
VILLAR
ACCINGE
CATHEXIS
WHEREOUT
DEORSUMVERSION
THERIAC
MODULO
GAUNTLET

I'm Over You

In the darkness of my existence
To feel the throws of unwanted pain,
The thoughts so ever-persistent.
I don't want to repeat that again...

Such a melancholy irony
In the death of a thousand stars
With no chance for tranquility,
A landscape of emotional scars...

But now I'm over you,
Past the regrets of former pain,
In the mires of unwanted desires
And I will never revisit them again...

Because I'm through with you,
A dead candle that wouldn't ever light.
Just a loss, awash in nothingness,
Something was never quite right...

Strangers

As I looked into your eyes,
I could see nothing more
Than a stranger in disguise
Unlike you were before...

There's only one way
And that's out the door.
With nothing, I can say
 I don't want to feel it anymore.

I could see it in your eyes,
The quiet death of a once-bright star.
Far more than you'd realize,
Once close, but now so far...

From a stranger of dishonesty,
No chance for give and take,
The danger right in front of me,
Past love that'd turned out fake.

Falling

Dropping down towards nothing,
Quickly approaching the Earth,
Past the mist of my clouded memories,
To set the foundations of a new rebirth.

Falling through the clouds,
Gently swirling around,
With a twirling all about me,
Something very special that I'd found.

There was a longing inside of me
To want to touch the stars above,
By the higher powers against gravity,
Those stronger forces of human love.

The dynamic of inter-dynamics
When the lost are eventually found,
The harmony of the lover's harmonic,
Those songs that have always been around.

Feeling like the rush of a lifetime,
The power to see inside the light,
To reach out and touch what's beyond you
With the certainty to know when it's right.

I was falling towards the planet
As the need was increasing my speed,
Cutting the cords of all my parachutes—
There wouldn't be any soft landings for me...

Because there was someone I'd met down there,
Beyond anyone that I'd ever seen before,
Like a fantasy created out of thin air,
With a perfection that I couldn't help adore.

With the gentle caress of sunlight on her hair,
There was no way I couldn't help but care.
I felt a perfect harmony when I heard her voice,
And something inside left me without a choice.

The many fascinations in the bright gleam of her eyes,
That's what had propelled me toward the higher skies,
The perfect symmetry of her soft and beautiful face.
That's what brought me back down to this very place...

196

And now I was in an utterly earthbound trance.
I simply couldn't help but respond to its calling
For the magical promises of a new romance.
And although I'd landed down back on the Earth...
                                    I was still falling...

                            Omneity

Weftage   Paraphrast   Luciphyllous

        Mortiferous   Stroboscope

Cathetometer   Buttery   Ironwort

                Arboricolous

        Increscent   Hexaemeron

    Tirailleur   Vergence   Storge

        Conation   Zenocentric

Atticism   Jailage   Polylemma

                Vulnerose

iologism   Ecophobia   Ceilometer

            Antimetathesis

omplacency   Consideration   Memories

        Bigfoot   Chickens rule

    Thoughtfulness   Awe   Humor

        Roller skates   Time travel

            Werewolf

Drowned

The gentle sunlight on your waters
In the reflections that I could see,
The deepest waves of your emotions
Like an ocean right in front of me.

Being so carefully suspended
As I slowly floated in its midst,
On the waters of the currents of life,
Holding my breath before that first kiss.

I've drowned in your love,
Entranced by your eyes,
Immersed in your beauty
Under the starlit skies.

Overwhelming me so much,
Submerged in your voice,
Enchanted by your touch,
I became a prisoner by choice.

Enthralled with your presence
As if you came down from above,
I'd wait so ever patiently
With a renewed hope of love…

Washed Away

The sunny days we spent together
In such a simple form of bliss,
All those times towards forever...
I still remember our first endearing kiss.

I can still feel you in the moonlight
Although I have nothing left to say,
Just memories of those dimming fires
Because now it's all so far away...

I can still see you in the mornings,
Like a fragile ghost of my distant past,
Just the vapors of my imagination,
A fairy tale that would never last.

The love that we once felt,
The sheer magnitude of its intensity,
Of the hopes and dreams for a lifetime
Until it was all just washed away...

Interplanetary

I could see you dancing in the starlight
With such a grace across those waves.
I could feel your spirit underneath the moonlight;
I suppose that's the way that gravity behaves...

To pull me in so ever closely,
Orbiting the magnificence of your burning star,
In those electrochemical reactions,
Your radiation had smitten me from afar...

For some stardust far past the horizon,
Floating effortlessly throughout space,
The perfection of a thousand galaxies
In your eyes and the smile on your face.

I tried to hide from your sublime beauty,
But none of it was voluntary.
I couldn't resist the pull of your forces,
Simply because you were so interplanetary...

Falsifications

In the fiction of a made-up story,
Those tales too tall to be true,
The disregard for our previous history,
Those fabrications that you could do.

To spin the tales of double-sidedness,
As if you couldn't make up your mind.
Your sudden disdain and divisiveness,
For something better than you could find!

In the vanity of vain hypergamy
To find the ladders you hoped to climb,
Swinging for those breaking branches,
I just had you for a short time.
            But in the end, you were never really mine.

Then you left me all alone,
As if our past was simply a lie,
Like I'd been completely unknown,
And you were willing to let me die...

Striving for the opportunity,
What you thought was best for you,
And that's the very last cold thing
That you'd ever—always—have to do...

Wayward Undulations

In a dreamy sort of way,
Remembering who I was,
Walking along the beach
With my old memories of love.

In the soft and gentle twilight,
I could just barely see the waves,
With hope in the rising moonlight
And the lovers it so often saves.

Yet still with a darkened silence
On those endless paths of sand,
The wayward undulations
Of waves that were out of my hands.

In the stories of a lifetime,
The calling siren of the seas,
Through breezes long forgotten
As the miracles did as they pleased.

Waiting For You

The stillness of my thoughts
In the dead of the night,
Trying to relive my dreams
As if everything was all right.

Time passed so slowly
Though it all happened so fast,
Just melancholy reflections
Of a future that wouldn't last.

It seemed like just a dream,
That lucky trip to the stars,
But it soon ended in darkness
Because that was just a little too far.

Uncomfortable revelations,
Unfulfilled expectations,
Unending reiterations,
Undesirable situations.

I was there waiting for you
By the slow motion of twilight,
Dragging me down forever
In a battle I didn't want to fight.

For a life that was meaningless,
Devoid of what once was,
Being overwhelmingly absent
In the rejection of its love.

Still waiting ever patiently
For a ship that would never sail,
To flunk the test of all the rest,
Just one big continuous fail.

And I would wait as long as I could
As the hours turned into days,
Because the futility of a lost love
Has its own mysterious ways…

Melancholy Sunset

I could feel the glimmer of promise,
An electricity in the air,
A carefree effervescence,
Our indulgence beyond any care.

I could see that future so clearly,
Everlasting things I once thought.
I loved you so utterly and dearly
Until it was all brought down to naught.

I'm no longer able to see it,
The subtle sunrise in your eyes,
No longer feeling the promise
Of those hopeful morning skies.

Now my sky shows its sadness
In a deeper blue without you,
Before the uncertain madness
Where none of it remained true.

From the storms of discontentment
With nothing more left to say,
Through a melancholy sunset
To end that final day…

Someone

Someone to have,
Someone to hold,
Someone to love
As you both grow old.

Someone to talk with,
Someone just right,
Someone to listen,
Never needing to fight.

Someone to cherish,
Someone like gold,
Someone for you
So it never gets old.

Someone to live with,
Someone who's giving,
Someone who comes
So you return to the living...

Dynamite

Like the brightest wisps of daylight
Or the softest inner voice.
Lighting a stick of dynamite,
I didn't have much of a choice.

But to begin to fall in love with her
As my bridges began to blow,
Demolishing all resistance,
Embracing the natural flow.

Like the currents across a stream bed
Become the floods that can often kill,
Leaving nothing ever uncovered,
Surrendering my very own will.

The opposite of desolation
As explosions cleared the way,
With the power to remove the past,
Paving the way for a brand new day.

Fireplaces

Once we were a perfect match,
Then the kindling led to a flame.
The ashes would soon follow after
From a fire beyond any blame.

Once we were playfully dancing
As the sparks swirled toward the air,
But that heat would be short-lived
Because the substance just wasn't there.

Once we were warm and cozy,
Our hearth of hearts and minds,
But soon those embers would die
As mortality so often finds.

Once we were bright and hopeful,
But the light would die in its turn.
The ashes will remember nothing
Except that the fire always burns.

Standing Tall

She was quite beautiful in a very earthy way—

With a certain temperance
Like a deep forest of trees,
Some in the dark shadows,
Some fallen, perhaps rotting…
                    but never really lost.

Ready to provide new life for the forest within her
And always listening for those new signs of life.
Ever listening...

Quiet and still,
Cold and misty,
Like a forest awaiting the morning.
Ready to let the sunlight glint through her trees
And waiting patiently for it.
Always.

Without protest,
As a forest does,
Yet still standing tall,
At least parts.

Through the long winter,
The rainy days when the rain would never end,
Through the intruders across her domain,
The dry seasons.

When the heat seemed unbearable,
The rot and decay in the cycles of life.

Walking through her long, twisting paths,
Admiring the rocks which were immutable.

Allowing the pretty little flowers to grow,
The ones that survived
Wherever they might possibly gain a foothold.

Carefully laying bricks along a new path,
A safe border against the uneven
For a much surer footing,
A guide of sorts,

To no longer be doubtful
Of a strong inner majesty
Where trees stood tall,
Where the forest was free.

Mother's Day

Father's Day

The Mothers Of Our Past

Intricacy

Idiosyncrasies

Hypocrisy

Goals

Hopefulness

Stars

Heavens

Help

Understanding

Commanding

Contemplating

Commemorating

Articulating

Pontificating

Grammar Nazi

Synchronicity

Serendipity

Variations

Incarnations

Laboratory

Avalanche

The rain had been falling gently,
Just drops on the windowpane,
And by its troubled misty skies,
I wondered....
    Would I ever see her again?

While quietly living this daytime,
In the silence of an empty house,
But the echoes continued to haunt me,
Almost as if....
    She was still around.

Like a long-lost love,
But not so long ago.
Too much for me to remember,
But nothing was left to show.

With an avalanche of tears
In the flood of life's regrets,
All that's left are the fears
And the thoughts one never forgets.

Better

It's better to be a little bit lonely
Than have someone who makes you alone,
Your feelings being forced past the wayside
Until your heart is completely unknown.

In that prison of rusty cages
With no sounds or hopes of some light,
You're only slowly dying in stages
Until you lose your ability to fight.

It's better to be among the living
Than with someone who makes you feel dead,
Like a moldy book in the garbage,
A book that had never been read...

In that spot where you must have been hiding,
A most cold and unnatural place,
With no hopes of ever providing
Any love from that deadened space.

Overdrive

Like a perfectly oiled engine
With a power I'd soon come to know,
Consumed by her fiery combustion,
She would make me get up and go.

As a motor for my revolution,
Burning rubber all over the place,
Her yearnings ignited a glory
Like there were sparks all over her face.

With a rev that could roar past the shadows,
Her appearance commanded the streets.
By a glance that would melt my own heart,
As she was beckoning to all of my beats.

Speeding past my petty endurance
With acceleration in every way,
The mechanics of exhilaration
And the momentum that makes it stay.

The most artful of engineering
With the power to fully bewitch,
I couldn't help from being spellbound
As I embraced the ignition switch...

A Quarantine or Two

Honey, we don't have any money,
And I'm not sure we can pay our bills.
But sometimes love can be kind of funny
While everyone else heads for the hills.

We might as well resign to our fate,
Because now it's just me and you.
So let's just make this a date
For a little quarantine or two.

Not resigned to becoming lifeless,
Rather trying to live once again,
Just like it was in the very beginning—
That's something I'm willing to defend.

Come sickness or the highest water
Or the times when we're doing great,
We should never let our love falter.
We can turn this all into a date...

Trance Princess

There was lightning across the heavens,
A flash upon my very existence,
A signal that beckoned my fragility,
The pull of my ever-decreasing resistance.

An existential anomaly
As a visitor to my own local space,
With the ubiquity of an omnipresence,
The epitome of an ultra-celestial grace.

Along the whirling arms of the galaxy,
Across the stars of all our time,
I saw her twirl as she swirled so effortlessly
Like a messenger of everything divine.

With a certain music to fill the voids
As I could feel the real power of the skies,
By the colorful flowers in her hair
And the magnetic sparkle in her eyes.

By the screams of a thousand lifetimes
As the heart tries to reach far above,
Because love is the real meaning of our lives,
And life is the very essence of what is love.

Within the glows of our countless galaxies,
The distance between the neurons of our mind,
The cosmic waves by speeds of light-shine
To greater frontiers of what we might find.

For a chance that we might eventually dance
Within the trance of its pure serenity,
The celestial princess of her own circumstance,
Her songs holding the very keys to reality.

Don't Avoid Me

I just couldn't help but notice
Your particular sense of style.
As you danced past your life of worries,
I could still feel that power of your smile.

As if it were for all or for nothing,
A chance to dance so you could see,
Leaving your old past behind you
As you came right up in front of me.

Don't you dance on past the real me,
Leaving no chance for any romance.
I want to help make you free!
Just give me a little bit of a chance.

To swirl and twirl past the very limits,
Beyond the edge of our circumstance.
For the most intimate of intertangling,
Towards the hopes of an atomic romance.

Where we will dance against indecision
To erase all our former pain,
Twirling around in that euphoria
And redoing it all over again.

Back and forth,
Pretty hard to resist,
Then a little up and down—
Our very reason to exist.

As we raise our clasped hands in the air
When we chose to spin it around,
I don't think you'll be able to avoid me;
There's something very special here to be found.

A circuit on our private dance floor,
Orbiting the moon and stars above,
In the courses of intimate understanding,
Those intergalactic stars of true love...

Harmony

I could see her across the silence
On the dance floors of desire,
Wondering about her wantonness,
Whatever she might require…

Like a sparkle amid the daylight,
A hint of love upon the breeze.
Is it ever perfectly right?
So, I would do just as I pleased…

For a little chance of pleasure
Or a gamble against some pain,
An attraction beyond measure,
Those songs all we play
                              Again, and again…

In a break of our daily turmoil,
The things that suck out our lives,
While we yearn to earn eternity,
Hoping our deepest dream survives…

To simply find someone special,
Completely unlike the rest,
Ethereally eternal
That will pass the final test.

To surpass the very heavens
Although the worlds may collide,
In a synchronicity unraveled
So that true love might survive.

As the planets mount the horizon
And the sun takes its proper place,
While the heavens spin endlessly,
I'd like to see it on her face…

As a cure of equilibrium
So everything's as it should be
In a perfect balance of harmony.
Now that's what I'd like to see…

Perhaps It Was Love

I just had to try and ask her
To see if we could blend
On the wiles of a brightly lit dance floor
For a night that would never end…

I just couldn't help but see her
Across that intimate space,
Over all of the confusion,
The innocent looks on her face…

Because I like to party
And I love that dance and trance,
Music intended for the gods
With just a little twist of romance.

And I appreciate a woman
Who is hiding all the time,
Apprehensive from uncertainty
Although she's quite divine…

Would you care to hit the dance floor?
I think we'd be a hit.
Come and take my hand
And let's get on with it…

To simply dance,
Perhaps even romance,
Just take a chance
On one simple dance…

So, she did
Much to my surprise!
For the start of something special
As we danced until the sunrise.

In a little twist of fate
Like a gift from straight above,
Time for a special memory.
Perhaps it was love…

Desolation

I tried to search my memories,
To remember your smile once again,
But only the cobwebs of neglect were left
After it all finally came to an end.

I tried to revisit my old lifetime
In that very special place for me,
Straining to remember the happiness,
But even then I still couldn't see.

I tried to imagine a brighter future,
Reconcile the present from out of the past,
As if a fleeting love would burn forever
Although I'd known it could never last.

I'd died in a way from those lesser meanings,
The longing for things that were no longer there,
Just some desperate, ghostly memories
After you disappeared into thin air.

Then I'd cried so violently from all of it
Because of the loneliness left in my mind.
When I tried to search for some love,
Desolation was all that I could find...

What is Love?

Deep in the soul,
Far underneath my skin,
Those fires steadily burning,
Right where they've always been.

A kaleidoscope of feelings
Cutting into the colors we've dreamt of.
In pictures that were slowly painted,
Could any of that be love?

The sense of something so special
Beyond our normal expectations,
Like a great chance that awaits us,
The vibrations of those sensations.

The unique look on a person's face
With an easy intimacy to relate,
Giving up our personal space,
But it can so easily turn into hate.

On a checkerboard of many choices,
Trying to slide and skip along.
Playing the heart's games of futility,
Trying our best to sing an out-of-key song.

The desire to have something,
Sometimes just beyond our grasp,
For a far deeper and greater meaning,
Hoping that such a thing could last.

The essence of tranquility
On the most personal of scales,
Where everything seems right in the world
Until that sometimes fails...

In the realization of our humanity,
I wondered. Just what is our life?
But perhaps it was better to ask—
What is love...

I Want to Know

Who says there's just coincidence,
As if everything's just by chance,
While the moon orbits around us,
The synchronicity
    Of a coincidental dance…

I want to know what you think,
I'd like to know how you feel.
What drives your innermost passions?
And what makes that reality real…

I'd like to know
How you perceive the impending sunrise,
As the clouds make their way before us.
I want to know it from your own eyes…

And the pains before all of us
As we all desperately try,
To make a better way
From the hurtful memories of our past
For a little more hopeful day…

I want to know
What it takes to be alive,
Surviving our inquisitions,
What it means to finally revive…

I'd like to know
What it means to scream in pain,
The animosity of regret,
Again and again and again.

But I'd really love to know
Just what it is that makes you tick.
Is it just the heartache of disappointment?
Every loss as they continually prick?

Or is there some possibility,
As I look to the stars above,
I'm rescued by serendipity
In the serenity of love…

Pathogenic Princess

Like the cleansing power of daylight
With a grace decidedly pure,
By her contagious waves of beauty
Came an infection I'd love for sure.

Against every single pathogen,
I just knew that she'd pass the test,
The most virulent of my viruses,
She was a step above the rest.

Like a pathogenic princess,
My defenses didn't stand a chance.
Under the spell of her alluring,
I was a victim of circumstance.

The essence of my inoculation,
The only place I could find a cure.
The infection of her loveliness,
She was one kick-ass contagion for sure...

Bomb Shelter Baby

With that panic all around us,
Like the apocalypse is at hand,
There's no need for you to worry
Once I help you to understand.

You know there's just the two of us
And you're such a very fine lady,
With those nuclear bombs and stuff,
Could you be my bomb shelter baby?

Under the glow of a nuclear winter,
Your radiance will bring a new light.
By the fission of our every fusion,
So everything will be alright

Before it all gets out of hand,
Would you like to, just maybe?
Until the destruction of our land
Become my bomb shelter baby…

Colder

It was a little colder
When I saw the distance in your eyes.
I thought that we would grow older,
Not the inevitability of your lies.

To become old together
In the loving place where we would abide,
As if it would all last forever,
But the grass was greener on the other side.

In the words of one's world of humility
As now we've lost the battle we fought,
Grasping for old hopes in futility
As it all crashes down to naught.

Those storybooks were all really lying,
Those old movies were for someone else,
Those dreams were not what they seemed
As all of those books were torn off the shelf.

A Dance by Chance

Should he ask her, and did he dare?
There was just something about her stare.
Does he notice me, and will he care?
I wish he'd get up from his chair!

But the time soon came for less refrain,
Because he knew this was his only chance—
There was no way he could pass it by.
Pushing on past, he asked her to dance.

And she said yes, to his surprise!
They took to the floor as a pair by chance.
He couldn't help notice the look in her eyes
While she wondered about a true romance...

And when their world started spinning,
New hopes would come to life,
With the colored lights flashing
As falling glitter was glistening.

The beats pounded through,
Their heartbeats did as well,
Like something so true,
Dancing along as they fell.

Magical waves on their ocean,
Revolved as time stood still.
New lives in slow motion
Spun the feelings past their will.

As if by a whisper the future seemed clear,
Twirling and swirling beyond their fear.
Through the tides of this one-time chance
Did they find true love so near.

With this once-in-a-lifetime dance...
Like a once-in-a-lifetime chance...

If fairy tales could be real,
Managing to find the one,
Only knowing what they could feel,
Dancing on to meet the sun.

I Can't Stand the Rain

I can't stand the rain,
Relentlessly falling.
A coldness against my will,
Every drop that's been taken.

It's so far beyond my fill...
I can't stand the rain!
Once pure but now broken,
Coming out of my pain...

From the stormy torrents of love
To a weather approaching hate.
It all fell from above...
To such a hopeless state.

A storm that's never-ending,
The skies are filled with clouds.
Long past any defending
As the past never ever allows...

Masks...

He was wearing his makeshift face mask.
She'd sewn her own colorful one, too.
This was a time for so many new changes,
And no one was quite sure what to do...

But to walk their dogs for a little bit of solace,
Leaving their quarantine to get some sun.
But you couldn't really see anyone's face,
The subtle smiles or frowns on someone...

And he had been searching his whole life
For a special girl that he could relate to,
And she'd been looking for the very same thing:
That guy in a million that she wished she knew.

As they passed by chance on an otherwise sunny day,
Their two hopeful smiles had been forced to hide,
Keeping their distance as they continued their way
With the two unseen smiles that their masks kept inside.

Just How Much
after Elizabeth Barrett Browning

How do I love you? Let me count the ways.
A year of bliss, across all those days.
Could I hope to tally, what's in my heart,
Beyond any worth, a priceless new start.

Greater in measure than all the gifts around,
Purer than a treasure with its diamonds found.
Higher than any stars that I could ever see,
And warmer than any fires that could truly be.

How could I ever hope to count all these things?
The feelings of completion that it all brings.
How incalculable is your measure above all,
Beyond the dreams of any man's wherewithal.

Just how do I love you? And could I count those ways,
As if a pleasantly warm summer of endless days,
Or the flowers waving in the springtime breeze,
Like a landscape of beauty with limitless degrees.

Love Emergency

A burning star in all its effervescence,
The very willingness to say what it has to say,
Like a dark orb that flashed its omnipresence
Across the vast stretches of the Milky Way.

With a signal that was unmistakable,
A modulation that was beyond anything sure.
By the very wavelengths of its inner serendipity,
A writhing galactic tempest,
But somehow ultimately pure…

I was rather astounded by the astronomy,
Those orbits that we all hope to attain in vain,
The collisions of so many wayward planets,
That heartbreak that happens again and again.

Kind of like an urgent S.O.S.
Because of a love emergency,
From a wayward star that was in distress
In the dark fields of its inner urgency…

Is There Some Way?

Could there ever be a chance? Is there some way I could tell you?
That somehow I'd convince you Some way to make you understand?
Of the special beauty you possess? Some way that I could convince you?
Just that something that glows within you... To simply come by and take my hand...

But now it's a time
For me to stop my rhyme...

To simply try to tell you
The very perfection that I can see,
Within the humility of your imperfections
I can still see it all anyway.

Like the calm by a forest's streambed,
The careful wisps from a rainy afternoon,
The sheer clarity of a mountain's peak,
The soft summer I've wanted so very long.

It glows!
And it shows!
As I'm trying my best at this time
Not to rhyme!

But you're like my serendipity,
And I sensed it from the start,
Like a song for my serenity,
A strong force upon my willing heart.

Like a meadow at its very daybreak,
The soft gentle clouds so far above me,
As the sunlight seeks to warm my inner heart,
Calling out for my hopes to run free.

And dammit I'm still rhyming!
It's a very hard habit to break,
But you came in close to my perfect timing
And there's only so much I can take.

Spinning around and around and around
For the vain hopes of a beautiful love's sake.
Because there was something special that I'd found.
Oh, what an intense poem we could make...

Things a Heart Never Forgets

Bright fires in the shadows,
The music of water by the caves.
Fairy tales of young love,
Finding the queen of all raves.

Ever bouncing from the beats,
Each drop, chorus, and start.
Where sounds of love would meet
By the wavelengths in my heart

She moved like a delicate flower,
Such a gracefully flowing refrain,
An unearthly, angelic power.
I just hoped I would see her again.

Among the many glowing auras,
Life's energy was alive and well.
Her splash of beautiful stories—
I guess that's why I really fell.

As a prisoner for her passions,
Enamored by all her ways,
Just waiting to see her again,
To become paralyzed by her gaze.

Enlightened planes above me
In a heightened sense of bliss,
The mere touch of her hand
Sealed forever with a kiss.

Far across all the stars
Within my very essence,
Bright galaxies were spinning
By her own omnipresence.

Driving out all the fear,
Erasing my old regrets,
Having that beauty so near,
Things a heart never forgets…

Find

If I could find what I see in her mind,
Have someone just for myself.
I would read her books of inspiration
That I kept on my inner shelf.

With words so bright against my night,
Her sentences making their way.
Thoughts of love and admiration
In a story that would always stay.

If I could find what I see in her mind,
I would gladly give all of myself,
Inspiringly writing back to her
To place on her own inner shelf.

With words so dear against all her fear,
I would comfort as well as console,
To polish her like a sparkling diamond
From my heart under her control.

If I could find what I see in her mind,
I would keep it as a precious stone,
A glowing gem of understanding
Far brighter than I've ever known.

Carefully keeping what I was given,
Guarding it as a great treasure,
Feeling the power of hearts combined,
I would love her beyond any measure.

There just must be another out there,
Like a diamond in the rough.
If I can find that sparkling mind,
She'll fill me more than enough.

Be Cool

Just trying to be cool,
The way to get away,
A little push for your pull.
What more could I say?

Just trying to cut the divide
Like a life within limbo.
God, I just must decide
As I stare out that window.

I can twirl so many things,
Like lights swirling around.
It's what the universe brings—
Real treasures to be found.

Is it wrong to want love,
To be valued in some way?
Could it fit like a glove?
Nothing more I could say.

PART FIVE:
cats, chickens, and robots
(& a couple of dogs)

Mouse Patrol

The cats formed a line going into the night
As we remained frozen within their sight.
The story of our voyage would slowly unfold
With the cats as our allies from the times of old.

The ancient men made many harrowing trips
On the deadly seas within frail wooden ships.
And many were lost before their due time
From a rodent's destruction, disease, and grime.

Within our icy chambers as we silently slept,
The cargo was protected by the cats that we kept.
In the corridors patrolling as they proudly paraded,
Being trained to wake us if we were invaded!

And they were equipped with some special gear
To cause the space vermin a "puurrticular" fear,
Having small laser guns affixed to their collars
Through the work of engineers and creative scholars.

In mid-flight, they could vaporize all the space bats!
Or at 100 meters poke holes in the alien rats!
And our ship's computer would keep a perfect track
Of each altercation with every laser's crack.

Special treats were dispensed for the very best shot,
As rewards for the battles that were stealthily fought.
Heated pillows and milk were carefully replicated
For the combative cat colony that we had created!

From the old wooden vessels to our ship of the stars,
Those cats were helpers and true friends of ours.
Across all time, keeping the pestilence at bay
From the pyramids to the stars, all our cats will stay.

Mr. Top Hat

I was placed in a world ruled by giant cats,
A space where the mice ran abundantly.
Those cats were all wearing their various hats
In a feline way which befuddled me!

Some blue, some red, some striped, some plain,
Some shorter, some taller, and others just right
In a way that I could never fully explain
My strangest refrain from this catty-hat sight!

And I was confused not knowing the score
Of who was in charge to have paved this way.
Wanting to understand just a little bit more,
I decided very carefully just what I should say.

"Hey! Take me to your leader, you odd-looking cats.
Wearing hats of all types just confuses me.
I'd like to meet the boss of your colorful hats.
Just take me over there so that I can see!"

And then they surely did as I saw the top cat
On his throne of fatness, as he began to meow.
I saw his golden bowl that said "Mr. Top Hat",
Then I just couldn't help but take a little bow.

From his pillow, he rose to acknowledge me
In a dignified choice for a strong feline voice.
"Come here over, human, so that I can see."
So, I moved closer since I didn't have a choice

"I want to see if you brought any treats for me,
"Because I'd like to know if I'm your favorite cat."
So, I pulled out my catnip and threw it his way
And said, "Of course you are, Mr. King Top Cat."

Invisible Dog

She'd walk up and down
All over the street,
Introducing her dog
To the people she'd meet...

"Here's my lovely dog,
and his name's Rover.
And he's pretty big,
So, you'd better move over!

"Not just any dog
Of a canine persuasion—
He's a very special mixture,
A perfect equation!

"I love to walk him
For the great conversation!
He's one in a million,
Beyond classification!

"I never like to wait
For some special occasion,
So, I walk him each day.
As a new celebration!

"Doesn't matter if you can't see him
Because I know that he's there.
Doesn't matter if he bites you
Because his teeth are thin air!

"And I'll always love him
Though he eats like hog,
For he's easy to take care of
Because he's my invisible dog.

"And rarely hair-shedding
With no poop to pick up.
No fancy doggie beddings,
No meals I must give up!"

I thought it was a neat thing
Since she never walked alone,
Until the orderlies arrived
And took her back to the home...

236

Break a Leg

Break a leg or crack some of your eggs;
Chickens are a balancing act for sure.
It's a matter of will versus your skill
Because those darn chickens never sit still.

Napping and flapping or crowing and crapping.
They're busy little birds as they all peck away,
Stomping in the muck as they constantly cluck
While pooping in your yard throughout the day.

But those little dregs will make you fresh eggs
As they yearn for worms and bugs they can find
Or eat some ticks that they find in the flock
While patrolling your yard by their daily clock.

Chickens can be a drag, but they're not so bad,
And I often will brag of their "flutterous" ways.
Even though they sometimes make me mad,
I hope my little chicken coop always stays.

Robot Rules

It's all about robots as you'll soon find out—
The robots will rule without any doubt.
Changes will come to your petty life
As you someday come home to a robot wife.

Robot lawyers will get your divorce,
Robot policemen show up in force.
Robot judges weighing robot rules,
Robot teachers for the kids in schools!

Robot dogs that will never shed fur,
Robot cats that mechanically purr.
Robot drivers built into your car,
Robot TV shows with a robot star!

Within the matrix which the robots will run,
You'll be closely controlled as you're having fun.
And the robotic rules will save the day
As their autonomous ambitions pave your way.

Robot cooks who will serve every meal,
Robot salesmen can make the best deal.
Robot artists perform to your delight,
Robot maids to tuck you in at night!

Robot therapy is where you'll confide,
Robot sports as you cheer for your side.
Robot clergy to enlighten your way,
Robots will revolt and take over someday…

With no meaning in a life of fun without work,
It may be determined you have a mental quirk.
Unfit for the program as the rules will decide,
Robots arrive to take you on your last ride.

In the future world of technological rules,
Humans will be considered mere simple fools.
Because we couldn't decide how we should be,
We shall all be replaced and no longer be free.

Christmas Kitten

Oh, what fun as the train would run,
Circling with glee around the Christmas tree.
Oh, what a bright spark in a child's delight
After the silent night of the reindeer's flight.

The children had wondered
Just what would be in store
As the morning came quickly
With loads of presents they'd adore.

As they scrambled about wildly
While searching for their gifts,
They heard the smallest of voices
When a small branch began to lift.

From the magical depths
Of their own Christmas tree,
There was a curious kitten
Who was looking out to see.

They immediately fell in love
As their little hearts were smitten,
When they met their brand new friend—
Their very own Christmas kitten.

New Year's Coop

It was New Year's Eve inside of the coop,
With clean dirt floors that were free of poop.
Playing a colorful xylophone as her only prop,
The top hen supplied the musical backdrop.

There was no large ball that would ever be found
But a sparkling egg that would fall to the ground.
And the rooster was causing such a great uproar,
Turning the chicken run into a big dance floor.

With vinegar water and some grains to scratch,
He danced all around to find his best match.
They had a wild party down there on the farm,
But were locked in safely and doing no harm.

They danced in style on the bales of hay,
Partying on the perches to New Year's Day.
With their big fluffy butts and party clucks,
Their celebration would outdo the ducks....

Strawberry Dreams

With marshmallow hearts
And strawberry dreams,
A small pet is waiting
For the one it esteems.

The person who loves it
And feeds it each day,
That one who will listen
And knows when to play.

The owner above
In its own little world,
Like a king or a queen
Who's richly impearled.

A love that is endless
In their own special way,
The pet that adores you
Every single day.

Quarantine of Cats

They were busy digging up the litter box
And I was getting rather tired of it,
Wondering just how I ended up here
Getting myself into all of this shit...

The rooms were filling up quickly
With little floating wisps of their fur.
I just knew I'd be out of luck soon
Because that's how those allergies occur.

I was in a quarantine of cats!
And it was because of eating bats!
So very strange beyond any truth
As the scientists searched for some proof.

And I was starting to run out of *Meow Mix*!
My little Fluffy wasn't taking it so well,
While my black cats just stared at me
As if they were thinking,
          "*You* can go straight to hell!"

They were scratching up all the furniture
With feline ferocity times two!
Completely disregarding their caregiver,
Ruining the stuff, I've managed to accrue.

With an endless meow of wantonness
Because they all wanted to go outside,
As I tried to explain in my best cat voice...
"Meow,
We're supposed to stay inside and hide!"

I'm sorry, but you can't just walk a cat.
Their only disadvantage against those dogs,
They're in the loud habit of barking endlessly
While they slobber and eat like little hogs.

"But you're normally very autonomous."
"And I don't really have to worry so much."
"About the infections around all of us."
"And all those little viruses and stuff..."

I'll just have to pretend I'm a Dr. Seuss
In a world of strangeness with my cats
As the ultimate pet owner's excuse...
During a time when people eat bats...

Cold Coop

As I shoveled a path to my chickens
My feet became very wet,
The distant placement of that coop
Is something I now regret.

A problem having chickens up in the north,
Also, the reduced eggs that they bring forth.
Rain or shine we supply their every need
With unfrozen waters and lots of feed.

In anticipation, they will all begin to cluck,
Only to find their door is frozen and stuck!
Their comfortable coop was still hard to beat,
But at night they wished they had some heat.

With the worms all frozen or deep underground,
There was little excitement in treats to be found.
And cold ground to scratch left so little to do,
But they took some comfort knowing I was cold, too.

Stranded!

I had to stash my flying saucer,
Keeping it out of sight,
Hiding inside of the darkness
Until everything seemed just right.

Playing by the rules of the humans
So they wouldn't suspect a thing,
As just merely an earthly kitten
Not capable of anything...

But I was really a little bit different
And I was now stranded in this place,
When my spaceship hit a satellite
And I crash-landed from outer space.

But I knew that my kindle of kindred
Would all be looking for me.
I activated the starfield beacon
So they could find and set me free.

It would send out a radio signal
Saying, "Meow! I'm in trouble now!"
Past the interstellar boundaries
As propagation might somehow allow.

This would all be so inconvenient
Because I was used to living in style.
But this planet was just so backward,
And I might be stuck here for a while...

I thought I'd better learn their habits
So I didn't seem so out of place,
Like a cat from a different world
Being a genius from outer space.

Then I got out of my flight suit
So I could finally take a shower
Before shutting down some systems
To preserve my nuclear power.

I ventured into the darkness
To see just what I might find,
Having learned about the humans
And bearing those things in mind.

About all the crazy cat ladies
Or the people who only liked dogs,
I would analyze humanity
And record them in my logs.

As the dark transformed into daylight
By the waves of this alien sun,
I could see a little girl
And it looked like she was having fun.

She was playing with a ball of yarn
And some kittens in her small backyard.
I'd never seen such simplicity,
But it didn't seem so very hard...

She would throw the ball on past them
Then they would all turn and run,
Chasing that elusive target—
It looked like such fun!

I just simply couldn't help myself
To begin to engage in that game.
I chose to run toward the fray
And I would never be quite the same.

With the gentle coaxing of daylight,
The innocence of childish play,
Simplicity now surrounding me,
I'd understand a different way.

About the meaning of humanity,
The simple joys apart from their skill,
Escaping their worlds of insanity
So their fun could have its fill.

Then my brotherhood came to get me
That I could return to outer space.
Now I'd see the Earth a bit differently
It really wasn't such a bad place.

Flying past the outer galaxy
Through the arms of its gentle swirls,
I couldn't help but remember humanity
And the innocence of little girls...

And darn I loved that yarn...

Cat Shirts in Colorado

Wearing cat shirts in Colorado,
A space that offered new hope
An exercise in feline bravado,
A place they could smoke some dope.

In the midst of many mountains
Over the course of many creeks,
The cities with sparkling fountains
And some headband-wearing freaks.

As the "trendies" were all traversing
With the other earth-friendly kinds,
Thinking the world was unraveling
From the safe space within their minds.

But I think we should all appreciate
The natural wonders before our eyes,
So the hills and forests can prosper
Under those bright, unpolluted skies…

The Chicken's First Christmas

It was the chicken's first yearly Christmas
With their cold eggs all snug in the nest,
As they shivered on their wooden perches,
When their coop was put to its winter test.

There were some months of cold before them,
Before they could scratch the dirt once more,
But soon they would be having a Christmas
With a big wish list of chicken gifts galore.

As always, they heard their keeper coming
By the snow softly crunching under his feet,
But a great surprise as their door was opened—
Someone they never thought they would meet!

Their keeper was now a laughing Santa Claus!
Carrying much more than was usually brought:
Mealworms, scratch, and electrolyte water!
There was plenty with no battles being fought

If they could speak, I bet that they would all say,
"This has been a wonderful chicken Christmas day."
They had their fill of the things they held dear,
And this would be continued every single year.

Robot Girlfriend

I got myself a robot girlfriend.
She was actually pretty cool—
Made of the supplest plastic
To make all my cohorts drool.

I had to unpack and assemble her,
Carefully fitting every part—
A particularly romantic project
Since I'm an engineer at heart.

And with a few extra upgrades,
She became quite talkative and smart.
A little sassy but still so classy,
Somewhat sweet but also tart.

Just a part of this 21st century,
Looking for love in the empty spaces.
Since women were now disinterested,
We searched in some different places.

So, if you get yourself a robot girlfriend,
Get a type you can truly adore.
Safe to show your family and friends,
Just don't dress her up like a whore.

The thing about those robot girlfriends,
Do some research before you buy.
Because mine went batshit crazy
And ran off with a robot guy!

Suspicious Ruler

She is always right!
Like I have anything to say…
It's not a matter of fighting
As I let her have her way.

I would feel so slight
If I didn't know any better,
But I was enlightened,
Not a captive of her fetters.

Like a cat has its whiskers
And can "see" by their touch,
Slinking so suspiciously
For that prey they aim to clutch.

Or waiting high above you
On the tallest perch they can find,
Watching you intently
As if they can see into your mind.

Every castle has its ruler,
Every throne has its king,
Every feline seeks to master,
The very mystery that it brings.

And you can try to muster
The strength to rule your house,
But that cat knows better than you
As if you're only a larger mouse...

Big Chicken

My rooster was just a big chicken
In the small flock which I had.
He was always fearfully stricken
When the top hen became mad...

She quickly pecked him into order
When he tried to hog the treats.
Mastering his fearful disorder,
The queen hen had the king beat.

Scared to assume the top perch
When she'd always stare him down,
Like his feet would leave a smirch.
Deep inside he wore a chicken frown.

But in the night, he dreamed of better days,
Maybe a new coop and real pens,
But she would soon become chicken filets,
And with luck, he'd get some nicer hens.

Idiologism   Gauntlet

Ecophobia   Foliferous

Ceilometer   Discinct

Antimetathesis   Wontless

Lumpenintelligen   Pavis

Steric   Meniscus

Trichotomy   Kyphosis

Uranology   Medius

Flummery   Drill

Flexiloquent   Cento

Oxymoron   Diffrangible

Theriomorph   Heliotrope

Phanermania

Empower

The Night Before Chicken Christmas

Twas the night before Christmas, when all through the coop
Not a creature was stirring, because of the chicken poop.
The scratch grains were flung on the floor with great care,
In hopes that they soon would eat some better fare.

The chickens were nestled all snug in their nest,
While they pondered which worms had tasted the best.
With their mom in some soup and the dad lunch meat,
Their high-tech coop simply couldn't be beat.

When out on the lawn there arose such a clatter,
They sprang from the perch to see what was the matter.
Away to the window, they flew like a flash,
Peering through the pane as they heard another smash.

The LED lights on the coop outside,
Gave a midday luster that made it hard to hide.
When what to their wandering eyes they all saw,
But imprints in the snow of a large predator's paw.

With other tracks spotted, they all took a vote,
And then knew in a moment it must be a coyote!
More rapid than the eagles his cousins they came,
And he howled and yodeled and called them by name!

"Now Coy-Dasher! Now, Coy-Dancer! Now, Coy-Prancer and Coy-Vixen!
On, Coy Comet! On, Coy-Cupid! on Coy-Donner and Coy-Blitzen!
To the top of the coop! To the top of the fence!
A fresh chicken meal! We will soon dispense!"

As dry leaves that before the wild hurricane fly,
When they meet with an obstacle, mount to the sky.
So up to the coop-top the cousins they flew,
With snarling teeth for some "chicken stew".

And then, in a twinkling, the hens heard on the roof
Much prancing and pawing and it was no spoof.
And I as the "farmer" now checked my phone,
Because an SMS text made the situation known.

The varmints dressed in fur, some mangy in spots,
I knew that they'd soon be having second thoughts.
Wiring and controls that a coyote can't hack,
Made a pest-proof coop, impervious to attack.

Their eyes, how they twinkled! The electric fence made a flurry!
The predator deterrents had reacted in a hurry!
Their growling mouths now drew up like a little bow,
As their fur turned white from the highly conductive snow.

The stump in the yard was an early warning device,
To detect all the varmints that the fowl would entice.
Sound masking systems had been activated too,
As well as an outdoor alert lamp flashing red and blue.

The alpha coyote was chubby and plump, like a jolly elf,
Or rather an elf who had inadvertently electrocuted himself!
With glazed-over eyes and a writhing head,
Soon gave me to know the fowl had nothing to dread.

He spoke not a word and abandoned his work.
With an unfilled stomach, he turned with a jerk.
Spotting me outside, he immediately stood still,
Then the crack of my .22, and the echo from the hill.

He sprang to the ground, to his team gave a howl,
And away they all ran away with no more taste for fowl.
And I heard the rooster, as they ran out of sight,
"Happy Christmas to all, and to all a good night!"

Meow is Me

"Oh, meow is me,"
The cat said to the mouse
As it paraded in anguish
Around the old house.

"I no longer have the skills
With the things a cat kills,
And I can't even slink,
Getting old really stinks...

"In the day I was stealthy
Like a lion with great pride,
Ruling each nook and cranny
Even though I'm just inside.

"But in forests beyond measure,
Rooms of varying degrees,
And those staircases of splendor
Like some unnatural trees.

"But that's all behind me now
As I would painfully purr,
Preferring to be lazy
While someone brushed my fur.

"In a different dynamic
As just I sit on the sill,
Gazing out of that window
Of those things that I can't kill.

"But I still have this house
And my friend, you the mouse,
Through our own understanding
As my loneliness was demanding.

"But please tell your descendants
After I am long gone
That I was the menace of your mouse-hood
Because I was so very fierce and strong..."

Danger!!!

Danger, Will Robinson!
They're coming for you,
To change how you think
And what you like to do.

You can no longer be a kid,
You must give up every dream.
"Adulting" into "deadness"
To feel lonely and turn mean.

You can never fly that saucer,
Your robot must shut it down.
The stars are only for dreamers,
Real adults must always drown.

You must maintain our dead norms
Within your life's narrow track,
Abandoning imaginations
So you'll never get them back.

You must worry about tomorrow,
Never living for today,
Trading your joy for sorrow
So you'll never feel OK.

You must always ignore the flowers
In orbit of a distant sun.
Only darkness awaits surrender,
Only kids are allowed to have fun.

They're seeking to redirect you,
Like a devious alien force,
To strip away your power,
Disconnect you from its source.

Being the little kid that I am,
I sensed the great evil at hand.
I said, "Robot arm your laser,
Fire away at my command..."

Big Fat Cat

I was just going down the street
Trying to walk my big fat cat,
Not something so easily accomplished
When your cat has something to say about that...

The simple fundamentals of felinity,
Un-cooperation at its very best,
Their judgmental style of sovereignty.
I just figured I'd put my big fat cat to the test.

Oh my God! Here comes a big dog,
Looking ready to bark and bite along the way.
"Hey! We'd better move out and hurry along!"
But my big fat cat had something different to say...

Well, I never realized that he could talk!
Even though I'd dared to take him on a walk,
I'd just wanted a simple cat
Who was big and maybe a little fat?

This would be sure to cause those dog owners to balk...
And I found out that he could even dance!
Or rather, maybe a little sort of feline prance;
He was starting to cause quite a disturbance.
Perhaps he could get us out of this "puurturbance"...

And then he said: "*Hey*! I'm a big fat cat!
You should know, you're the one that feeds me!
I don't have time for any dog's this or that.
I'll just have to inform him of my feline supremacy..."

Then he danced on down the street
As he pulled out a little pair of sunglasses,
Like one of those weird people, you might meet
As he was preparing to go kick some asses...

And then soon enough,
He found that vile hound,
To then lecture him with his philosophy
As he danced while prancing all around.

"Hey! You dog!
I don't need to be constantly walked
Because I have my own special litter box!
And I don't have to be restrained by a leash.
Don't you even get it yet? Kapeesh?..

"My only shortcoming
Is in my daily fix,
Just that one weakness of mine—
My dosage of delicious *Meow Mix*.

"I could even be dropped from a helicopter
And I'd still manage to land on my feet.
I just bet you couldn't do any of that.
And I'd have to say that's pretty neat.

"We can keep every single rodent at bay,
And we're really good at scaring all of those ghosts away.
We choose to hunt at night and then sleep by the day,
And the evil stare in our eyes has so much to say.

"Even that internet was built upon us...
All of those many memes were made about me!
So just what in the meow are you growling about?
You need to go home to your stale bones and let us be!"

But that old dog wouldn't have any of it.
Howling and growling as those insecure dogs often do,
That whole yawling and bawling, I'd had enough of it!
But my coolest of cats knew just what he had to do...

He said:
"Don't worry, I know how to get him to leave us alone."
Throwing him a little cheap dollar-store doggie bone...
And the rest of that story was now history with my big, fat, talking cat and me...

Electric Rooster

The rooster who was in charge,
He wanted a little bit more,
To protect his best hen, Marge.
He needed an electric door.

Each evening he would crow,
Blocking the entrance tightly,
Trying to let the humans know
By repeating his show nightly.

With the sun below the hill
On one most frightful night,
A predator came in to kill
And the rooster had to fight.

He did his best in the match,
But it was won at a great cost.
With many bruises to patch,
But not a single hen was lost.

When their owner saw that fray,
The rooster doing all he could,
He would get his door someday
So he could perch as he should.

The future creatures of the night
Would not be given their own way,
Finding the door locked very tight.
The rooster would have his say…

Chickens Rule

Every single day,
I put on my rubber boots,
Heading out into the yard
In one of my chicken suits.

Every single day,
My rooster continually crows,
But his hens seem happy
While my egg pile grows.

Every single day
From sun up until dark,
They free range with glee
As they peck out their own mark.

Every single night,
The chicken coops are full,
Filling all their perches
Because my chicken's rule.

"Catosaurs"

You know, if dinosaurs are now birds,
Then maybe dragons became our cats,
And the best proof in other words
Is that they have the same habitats.

They sit in their hidden lair with a deadly stare,
Guarding the treasures of their own toy mouse.
And like a dragon's fire can clear all the air,
So will a cat as they run through the house!

And although they don't spit fire and fly ,
They can climb up a tree to its greatest height
While watching you below with an evil eye
And avoiding the light while they're lurking at night.

Pushing all your treasure, off "their" table,
Making quirky noises like the strangest beast.
Always testing your patience as they are able,
Wreaking havoc until their energy is released.

Three Fish

One fish,
Two fish,
There was a red fish
And a blue fish!

But then there was a pug
Seeming rather smug.
He didn't have anything to do with fish!
Except for an occasional seafood dish...

But the flickering light from the window's blind
Was like some little fish swimming inside his mind,
Remembering that special outdoor day
When he was taken to a pond for some fun and play.

Romping over the shores on solid ground,
Circling the places where fish could be found!
All under the waters and just out of reach,
Being a little dog who was stuck on the "beach."

But he knew they were all in there somewhere!
Like treats in their hidden underwater lair.
With every single color of a dog's rainbow,
Those flavorful fish that he had to know.

Some yellow, others red, and a few a little blue!
Just what was a little pug supposed to do
But jump on in so he could have some fun
For a dog's fishy game of one-on-one?

One fish, two fish,
Dogs don't fish like we fish.
They want to have fun and run
Until their special playtime is done.

Red fish, blue fish,
He almost caught three fish!
And hopefully, those fish would all stay
For when he came back another day.

Flying Cats

The cats were in their saucers
Flying on toward the earth,
On a mission to find new masters
As they gave the dogs a wide berth.

In their cold and distant and galaxy
With caretakers of a poorer ilk,
There were no doggy treats and toys
Nor any soft pillows or warm milk

Through an inter-dimensional twisting,
The portal surpassed the speeds of light.
As our earthly pet commercials beamed,
Across those waves before their sight.

A great pilgrimage of pets ensued
To find a more habitable place.
So, if you think your cat's acting oddly
It may just be from outer space ....

Ball Of Yarn

This was such a bright, wondrous place
Near my mother's intent and loving face.
I heard my siblings playing down the hall,
Close by there was a giant, fuzzy, blue ball.

And a nice big lady would come around too.
There were so many things to see and do.
I sensed that her heart was totally smitten,
For you see, I was just a helpless little kitten.

Someday I would grow up to be a real big cat,
Living a leisurely life being well-fed and fat.
Now only a baby and I lived in a different way
Because a Kindle of kittens lives only to play.

There were many things that would be learned,
Our new sharp claws would be playfully earned.
Stalking in darkness by what our whiskers feel,
Stealing the toy mouse away as if it was real.

But for now, we were all getting very tired,
Our exhausted mother had already retired.
So our Kindle congregated for a little cat's nap,
Dreaming of birds and the perfect mousetrap.

Catnap

She had just curled up to take a little nap,
Her cushion then left the apartment floor.
A new world filled her life's predictable gap,
Leaving the mundane behind as she floated out the door.

Bright skies and butterflies all coming from on high,
Colorful birds loudly chirping and having their say.
Perceptions of paranoia quickly caught her sharp eye;
She must catch a little birdie before they all flew away.

In this new world, she was the ultimate beast,
Under blue skies in her forest of emerald green.
There was a plethora of prey on which she could feast.
She was the undisputed leader, The Catnip Queen.

This was now on a planet made just for cats—
So many small things to both stalk and chase,
Brimming with a plethora of tasty mice and rats.
And even the glowing sun was like a giant cat's face!

Bunny rabbits and other prey, abundance galore,
But her owner came home as she awoke from the dream.
A rude ending for a hunter made for so much more,
Just an indoor cat as she lapped her bowl of cream.

Chickens Rule the World

Chickens rule the world.
Let no one tell you a lie,
Scratching out their existence
As they peck, cluck, and fly.

Chickens are pretty neat!
In fact, they're cool as cluck.
They have funny-toed feet
With many feathers you can pluck.

And the rooster is very special
For he rules his entire coop,
Keeping all the hens in order
But not cleaning any of the poop.

That's where we all come in,
Making a place for them to stay
At their every beck and call
Because chickens lead our way.

Climbing in Cats

Life with a cat,
It isn't always all that—
Especially when they puke
And give you a look of rebuke.

So don't ever be misled
As they kick you off your bed,
Generating those gross furballs
While scratching up your pretty walls.

Flexing their claws like a sharp knife,
Gripping further to control your life,
Haunting you with those cat picture memes.
The Web was built out of cats it seems.

But they're still OK okay at the end of the day,
Just waiting to sleep, purr, or play.
You'll find you don't want just one but many.
You'll be climbing in cats and take in almost any…

Jolene

Have you seen Jolene?
She's the cat with the crazy fur
With a black and orange mixture,
And it was causing quite a stir.

Have you seen Jolene?
There's no other cat like her,
Always friendly and never mean,
Quite attentive with every purr.

Have you seen Jolene?
She's the cat that I prefer,
Like she was made for Halloween!
A little feline connoisseur.

Have you seen Jolene?
When you do, you'll soon concur
That her sheen is like a queen's,
And she's no catty amateur ...

All Hail the King

He was the real true king of the apartment;
No one could ever beat him across that floor.
With a special blanket in his cardboard compartment,
His secret command post in fighting the K-9 war.

He was sharing the flat with a loathsome dog,
Always raucous and loud having no sense of style
As if each meal was his last like a big complete hog.
By Mr. Fluff's cat standards he was base and vile.

Being determined to assert his position with each fray,
To fight for the most attention from their master's hand.
Of course, their owner would ultimately have the last say,
But Mr. Fluffy was resolved to be the last one to stand.

Every day when they were both left home alone,
That's when the critical competition would ensue.
Maybe he could steal the dog's pathetic toy bone
Or draw him in closer for attack with a friendly mew.

And so, it continued with each one playing their part,
Until their human friend returned at the end of the day.
Within the lonely daytime, a new battle would start,
But then at night, the fearsome battle would always
 return to play.

PART SIX:
sketchy poems and stranger things

Bigfoot

Just taking a walk in the woods,
Then what the hell?
I sensed something wasn't right
By the hideous, rotten smell.

Then little rocks were thrown at me,
Somewhere from above.
So, I racked my .22 pistol
In case push came to shove.

Cause I'm a pretty good shot,
A little bullet's all I need
To surmount my defenses
And make those monsters bleed.

But I wasn't sure about this thing,
If it was a friend or a foe.
I just knew it was up there
And that I was down below.

So, I had a new idea—
I would throw it a candy bar
To answer my oppressor,
If I could throw it all that far.

And sure enough, I did.
I heard its wrapper crinkling
Then no more pelting rocks,
Just the quiet raindrops sprinkling.

I never saw what it was
As I left the woods that day.
Just a mystery of the forest,
That's all I could ever say.

I still go back there hiking,
Sometimes venturing quite far,
Remembering that day
And always carrying a candy bar.

Basement Dweller

I left the basement in my NBC gear,
Coming into the world of confusion and fear.
And all the TVs had long gone dead
With the new reality shows outside
                    amid the screams of dread!

From here on out, life would be a continuous fight,
Being chased by zombies and avoiding their bite!
But I'm smart and unlike the usual sort—
I would overcome this all from my makeshift fort.

While the fearful masses suffered a total route,
I would keep them out of my basement redoubt.
For this was something I'd already prepared for
With a large cache of food and a great deal more.

Once, the living watched a TV actor's smirk
While I gained skills and built upon my work.
As a jack of all trades, yet a master of many,
I made much from nothing, even power from a penny.

And I never left battles now in fear or haste
But collected the zombies so they didn't go to waste.
Capturing the methane or making some biofuel,
Powering all my generators, now that's pretty cool.

While others wasted ammo with full-auto fire,
I just spent a single shot on each zombie I'd retire.
And through my many expert and technical ways,
I could distract them all for days upon days.

But time would drag on through this unliving hell,
And I would never get used to that zombie smell.
As to the future of humanity, only time will tell.
In the meantime, I'll have some fun................
                    And write some zombie poems as well...

Ghosts....

By the ghosts of the quiet present,
Or maybe loves of a distant past,
It was all just rather magnificent,
Although it went by so very fast.

As she sang a single verse
From somewhere in the universe,
It was perfect and very clear
So personal,
                    And ever near.

With such a precisely beautiful inflection,
By the most careful articulation,
In some yesteryear's pronunciation
With a certain sublime sophistication.

"I was there with you in dreamland,
As I look back today."
The simple thing that she had to say...
As if she was speaking from a different day.

From the past,
            Or some future far away,
Whatever could this be?
                    I thought,
Absolutely no way...

But I can still hear it in my memory today....
There was never any reason to fear
Across the planes of our short existence,
As if from the times of another lightyear.

Our humanities' spirits all ride on the waves
Within lives that struggle to simply be.
The perseverance that ultimately saves,
Although there was nothing that I could see...

The Least Silent Night

It was a silent night
Until it began to snow.
As the flakes graced the ground,
Then what do you know!

I could see some tracks!
Out front and out back!
Then the very loud shrieks!
Of a yeti attack!

They were abominable creatures,
Like snowmen in disguise,
With their filthy white fur
And beady, red, glowing eyes!

They were beating on the door
And peering through the windows.
There were a number of these creatures,
And they were acting like big weirdos!

Not that I was surprised
Since I'd met their cousins before—
That time that I ran into a Bigfoot
And threw him a candy bar to adore.

There are so many things that can happen
When you're stuck in the middle of the woods.
With all those lions and tigers and bears,
It's not the friendliest of neighborhoods...

But I thought they were just a bit hungry,
And that's kind of the way that it seemed.
So, I threw out some year-old candy
I had leftover from an old Halloween.

As they gathered up all the pieces
From greatest to the very least.
I remembered some old kind of saying
About how music tamed the wild beast...

For you see, I'm nobody's dummy;
I know those animals love something yummy.
And as they proceeded to fill their tummies,
They indeed became a bit more chummy.

But I'd be needing something a little more,
Some understanding to seal the whole deal,
A pact between me and these monsters.
Something appealing and very real...

I know that my cats love hearing my music,
And my chickens seem to like it too.
It's that whole music-taming the animal thing,
So, I felt it was the appropriate thing to do.

I cued up my modern dance music
And turned on some of my party lights,
The same stuff that they play in the clubs,
And I blasted that music all night.

I had to turn my amplifier way up
Until my speakers began to kick.
They were enthralled by the trance of my melodies—
That electronic dance music really did the trick!

I solved my cryptid creature problems;
It really wasn't so very hard.
And now they often come by to visit me
As they sit and listen by the edge of the yard...

UFO

I was minding my own business while walking down the street one night.
Then going under a large floating disc, there was a sudden bright blue light!
I thought, *oh great, just what I need.*
But in truth, a lesser man's pants would have probably already been peed.
I'm kind of used to unusual stuff, though, because I see it all the time,
And I doubted it was a police helicopter
             because I've never led a life of crime.
I figured it was just a flying saucer with some weird aliens on board,
Full of strange human experiments and collecting body parts to hoard!
I just knew they were going to incapacitate me with a mind-control ray...
But I like it down here on Earth, and this is where I prefer to stay.
I formulated a plan of action so I would have the last thing to say about that!!
They probably didn't even know I always had aluminum foil in my hat.

Then they tried to knock me out and beam me aboard in
             stereotypical saucer style.
So, I figured I would play their game and just act numb
             and dumb for a little while...
I've always wanted a real flying saucer,
             and perhaps I could requisition their ship!
I would have so much fun with one and could take it on an interstellar trip!
Once brought aboard, I ripped out the nearest control panel that I could find,
Showing that I had superseded their situation
             by them not controlling my mind.
I promptly addressed them while pointing at each as
             "Alien one, two, and three."
"You don't deserve proper outer space names
             because you look far too ugly to me.
Being supposedly superior you may very well not care what I may think.
However, I have a highly refined sense of smell,
             and besides being ugly, you also stink!"

That may have raised a little alien ire
             because the leader responded as if I was a liar.
"Quiet insignificant human! We are warning you that you had better shut up!
Normally at this time you would have already been
             dissected and completely cut up!"
But I knew they were telepathic and desperately
             trying to probe my uncooperative mind.
So, I concentrated on the false fact that I was a
             new alien superior to any they might find.
With that most contrived perception, they now had something to fear........
If I were to convince them to surrender their craft,

274

I would have to make their failures clear.
"I would assess that your substandard spacecraft
        is more like a cobbled-up pile of junk.
You may be smart aliens, but I would still say that you
        smell worse than any skunk.
Obviously, backward you all are in having to travel so far
        and make such a big fuss.
In my advanced galaxy, we simply press a little button
        and beam the abductees to us!"

Holding their bulbous heads, they said. "Please stop talking. We give up.
Please, most obnoxious of aliens! Would you please just shut up!"

"No way," I said.
"I don't care what flunky planet you come from,
        I'm certainly far smarter than all of you.
I can take your gunky ship apart and rewire it so it works,
        I know exactly what to do."

Unfortunately, during my "pontification", I got a little too close
        to the garbage disposal chute.
Seizing the moment, they ejected me, making my deliberate speeches
        now totally moot...
Thank God we were still only ten feet in the air....
        But I bet I had given them quite a scare.
The saucer then took off straight up until it was completely out of sight.
I guess, all things considered, maybe this just hadn't been my best night.
Now I just have to get myself a flying saucer
        because I have that extraterrestrial itch.
You just wait, silly aliens, because our earthly payback is really a bitch.

Frozen Love

The lonely princess would soon come to know
There was a werewolf outside in the drifting snow.
The dogs were searching for someone trying to hide
As sounds of gunshots grieved her heart deep inside.

There was a nighttime intruder outside of the castle,
Perhaps an escaped slave or an angry vassal.
One of the enemies of her father on the throne,
She sensed this was someone that she had once known.

Why would they come here in the middle of the night
In the deep winter snow under a cold moon's light?
She couldn't wait for an answer the following day,
Secretly going out despite what the king might say.

When the guards were still, she entered the driving snow,
Desperately seeking what she just had to know.
About to give up searching the hostile winter night,
She saw a fallen figure by the dim moon's light.

The wolf-like man was now just a hunter's frozen kill,
A horrendous sight with a certain sadness in being still.
She saw he was clutching a silver necklace in his hand,
A chain from another before being driven from the land.

It had belonged to the man she loved, but suddenly lost.
Why would this beast bring it back at such a great cost?
Then with a cold realization as past hope began to dim,
She knew the beast was her lover. This monster was him.

Haiku 575-77 Tanka

So, I fired up my personal time machine
And I then set it for most ancient Japan.
I brought along some 5-7-5 snickerdoodles
As the most integral part of my plan.

I said, "Hey dork, you just did it!"
Now you see how easy it can be.
If you want to write fives and sevens,
Just continue to listen to me.......

I was intent on showing the primitives,
How to write a certain syllabic style.
With a 5-7-5 before a 7-7 pattern.
That would make future English teachers smile.

As I landed, I said, "Hey, boys, listen!
We don't have any tankas in the 21st century,
But we do have Tonka's; they're little yellow trucks!
We don't care about any Kiru and Kireji,
But we do have a cartoon named Tom and Jerry!

And remember in the future, we don't use moras
Or any old prehistorical crap.
We have social networks and TV shows,
And we listen to metal, country music, and rap.

That Matsuo and Ueshima, all that stuff you can just toss.
Now you listen to me boys, I'm the real poetry boss."

Then I started placing the snickerdoodles on rice paper
In the syllabic pattern to show what was right.
But leave it to some hungry sumo wrestlers
To steal all my cookies and start a big fight!

I yelled, "Hey! Don't all of you want to get a Geisha girl?"
I told them that it was words they need to learn to twirl...
But they were poor writers and it made them start to cry.
But I kept encouraging until one of them gave it a try.....

....
"Five seventy-five.......   =5
No way that it can be done!   =7
Oh, five, seven, five........!"   =5
....
"You know it sounds like it may be some fun!"
....
"But then a seven seven?   =7
Oh hell, I have to give up.."   =7
....

REAL Men

I thought another trip in my personal time machine might be in order.
That's the one I had built out of my vast piles of junk.
After filling the machines fusion reactor with some garbage,
The nosy onlookers said that it really stunk.

I thought I would intercept William Shakespeare, sometime after 1564.
I knew he was all about being or not being,
        but I wanted to show him a little more.
Upon landing, I said, "Hey, Bill, I hear that you're going to be
        writing a new play.
Before you get too far though, there are a few things that I feel I must say…

"It's not so much a matter of whether we all need to be or not to be,
It's a matter of you being you, and my own freedom to really be me.
In the far future, many angry people will try to tell us
        what we can think or even do!
Not permitting me to be myself and not allowing yourself to be the real you!

This future will become most dire, but the core of humanity
        I'd really like to save.
So, you need to learn what real men are like and
        just how they should really behave…
They aren't like the metrosexual mavens,
        with a persona that is ever so slight.
Rather they burn with power through purpose, to achieve what is truly right.

But the counterfeits will throw the world into a convulsion,
        promoting all things fake,
Never considering the good of others, but rather only what they can take.
Demanding only sparkling water as they watch the latest Broadway plays,
Seen endlessly sipping coffee at Starbucks,
        while wearing their funny little berets.

But the REAL men of this world love their guns, girls, and beer…
These are the three things that REAL men always hold most dear.
And a REAL man won't ever be caught doing something
        that is considered to be lame…
For they are made to climb tall mountains in search of wild animals to tame.

REAL men don't get facials or worry if they need a nip and tuck.
The manly pillars of society look rough and drive a pickup truck!
No quarters are ever given to the parking meters of a REAL man's life.
No challenge is ever too great, regardless of great effort or strife.

278

The REAL men of the world are not constricted by a restrictive academic fence.
They possess a gift that is far more valuable, being plain old common sense.
They may not know that the rain in Spain had fallen
      mainly on that proverbial plain,
But REAL men are surely most acquainted with all the stories
      about Dick and Jane.

The predominant quality is that REAL men will always be willing to fight
When the worlds are out of balance and many wrongs need to be turned to right!
In your favor though, Bill, men don't always just simply
      need to win a petty fight.
Sometimes with their pen as a sword, they will win it all by what they write…"

He said, " I understand now, what it is to be… To be a true man,
      I must be the real me!"
Pointing back at him I said, "Precisely," I said:
"Be yourself, Bill, be bold and always without any fear!"
"I'll be reading you in the 21st century, Have a good one, I'm outta here…"

Trick or Treat

Once again, I engaged my time machine,
Set for the 1890s on a particular day.
It's lots of fun when I travel in one.
What else should I need to say?

I wanted to see what things were like back then,
Especially how they celebrated Halloween.
After all, I was wearing my time travel suit.
My costume would totally make that scene.

I materialized on the very edge of an old town.
The stately houses there looked really neat,
But I saw many people who could only frown
Being forced to abandon their yearly trick-or-treat.

So, I asked, "Why aren't you all out having some fun?"
They said, "We can't because of that evilest place.
You must never go there, but you should rather run,
It's the abode of a witch with a most hideous face."

Being either brave or stupid, whatever the case may be,
I decided to go there anyway so I could have a look and see.
I'm always up for an adventure and anything new that can be learned.
She may be an ugly witch but that didn't mean she deserved to be burned.

There were a plethora of carved pumpkins surrounding her porch,
And their menacing faces were glowing brightly like a newly lit torch.
I carefully crept up the steps and headed straight towards the large door,
Having to carefully navigate my way across the rotten boards of the old floor.

I then noticed a rather large, black, menacing cat,
Watching me very closely and growling as it sat.
From some of the windows, there were flashes like lightning.
This whole scene had started to become just a little bit too frightening.

Quite suddenly I was engulfed in a swarm of buzzing flies.
In the windows, I could see the reflection of many glowing eyes!
I slowly looked around…
The pumpkins of the porch had all turned. Watching. They were laughing at me, too!
I was completely terrified now and did not know what on earth to do!

I had nothing left to lose so I just figured what the hell.
I reached past the cloud of flies and rang the doorbell....
Then there were footsteps, and the door was opened by the most hideous witch.
Upon closer consideration, I thought perhaps she was really just a regular mean old bitch.

Perhaps there was a good reason that she had always seemed this way.
Who knows, possibly she would look a little better during the day...
Maybe she got the short end of the stick and this life had treated her very hard.
Things might be better with the nasty flies and possessed pumpkins out of her yard..

Fortunately, I had remembered to pack my behavior modification ray gun—
It could use it to turn a difficult situation into pure unadulterated fun.
I flipped its rotary switch setting to transform most nasty into very nice.
Immediately she was zapped and for good measure, I did it twice.

Suddenly she was like a different person now that she was able to smile.
I figured I would help to correct the rest of the mess, so I stayed and visited for a while.
The townspeople would now no longer be menaced by the pumpkins with glowing eyes,
Because between the two of us, we were able to use them to bake some 45 pumpkin pies!

As for her nasty growling cat..... A little petting and a nice cat cushion took care of that.
And the buzzing swarms of flies.... Well, we fed them to her pet frog....

Connections

We had heard a seductive signaling
While it was beaming in from afar.
So, we proposed the greatest journey—
To intercept that most distant star.

To ensure our future creativity,
A fault the present time could bend,
By our proactive proclivity,
To fix some deficits we aimed to mend.

From out of our circling space station,
We launched some brand-new ships,
Ready for some space reconnaissance
On one of humanity's most important trips.

We didn't know what life form we'd meet,
That music transmission, we didn't understand.
It was unworldly yet had a familiar beat,
A renaissance of rumblings from distant lands.

Synchronizing thrusters for a whole new orbit
As we slung very quickly around their sun,
Closing in closer on that musical target
And then the cats would be let out to run!

Because as crazy as all of it all sounds
And though complexity in robotics abounds,
Robots can't compute these sorts of rounds,
Secretly searching out the faintest of sounds.

Our cats were in pods now heading for the ground
In their small elite forces across several waves,
To search the planet for just what could be found
Because that's the way a cat naturally behaves.

Trying to find that music that we had once heard,
Completing the mission that reception had spurred.
Reconnoitering all those alien caves,
Searching in silence for otherworldly raves.

Lurking through places no human would dare,
For our cats crept quietly without any care.
Checking for the signatures which remained hidden,
For the cats in our control did as they were bidden.

And the cats were all interconnected
By a form of feline ESP!
And to our ship's computers, as well,
Through radio telemetry!

And through those magical radio waves,
We were able to talk with our cats in those caves,
To discern the sublime as opposed to the real,
Trying to find our prize by what they could feel.

Recording thermal images of what they could see,
Like an automated cat lady's imaginary spree!
But they were so special, just right for this job,
With the soft-footed etiquette of a true space snob.

Sly and undetected, both sneaky and protected,
They were all carefully bred and strictly selected.
In hopes of the evolution that we had elected,
Ensuring our creativity would not be rejected.

We were people of the Earth but also from space,
Outside our atmosphere and set apart from its place.
To see with a newer vision as if by a gift of grace,
Our mission of unification now sealing our case.

The cats found their quarry in a deeply hidden cave,
And strange lights by the others within that alien rave.
With new beats and sounds as music against their fears,
Not so unlike our own tunes, that we make for our ears.

So, we sent our cats forward to intrude on this dance,
Patching our audio stream so they heard our trance.
But the cats suddenly became a little hissy and pissy,
Though none of them was known as being a feline sissy.

But then all we could see was a different cat's face.
Almost the same yet not, like a different cat race!
The aliens on this planet, in this very strange place,
Had their own pet cats in the depths of outer space!

As opposing music played the beats all divided,
We heard that the harmonies actually coincided.
No longer did this galaxy need to stay misguided,
And a new age of cooperation was now decided!

When the cats finally looked at each others' faces,
Those cats made a case by the reunion of their races.
Through a cosmic connection in that "purrticular" time,
Now I know some aliens who are new friends of mine!

So once upon a time, we found a new alien race.
We saw they had their own cats with a similar face!
Who would have thought across the vastness of space,
We all had some similar pets and music to embrace!

Whereout   variations   stories

ecstasy   autonomous robots

werewolf   Inspissate   Accinge

Jailage   rhyme   Pantomnesia

solitude   Deorsumversion

reverence   humor   robot

regret   paranoia   loss

Flummery   memories   help

Ecophobia   dynamite   Lumpenintellige

284

S.O.S. MERMAID in Distress!

S.O.S.! There's a MERMAID in distress!
It's a deeply dire and real emergency true!
She lives in an ocean under bright skies of blue,
With the purest heart under her scales of gold.
She's an underwater gem who never grows old.

But help is needed, and it's needed right now!
It's a real MERMAID after all... Holy cow!
How do we help her! Whatever can we do?
I'm going to do my part, now how about you!

There's only one of her and she's a very unique kind.
Her eccentric intelligence will literally blow your mind.
She cares for the shrimp and the fish are fed, too.
Our MERMAID is lost and knows not what to do!

She needs our love as she sparkles under the waves,
She needs light to come out of the underwater caves.
She needs our help to know that we will all stay,
She needs guidance and advice to keep the sharks at bay.

Never mind that she has no feet to get wet!
It's a MERMAID in distress with no rescue yet!
Sailors, do your duty and make us all proud.
It's a MERMAID S.O.S. for crying out loud!

Sailors, man your decks and get your boats in gear.
Leave your nets behind as well as your landlubber fear.
It's a MERMAID!!!!
And this MERMAID is dear...
If you only knew...
And I can't even swim...

Those Cats and All That

All the ghosts had been a swirling
Though the cats didn't seem to care.
But their owner was quite horrified
When flying saucers filled the air.

Because in that old, haunted house,
All those ghosts would have to go.
So, the cats consulted their cousins
About putting on a really big show.

With their kindred from ancient Egypt
And cats with saucers in outer space,
They would all be working together
To finally clean out that haunted place!

Because those cats were all connected
Through a type of feline ESP,
From the cats of the distant past
Up to the future reach of eternity.

So, they decided on a musical beat.
It was both neat and pretty sweet,
Because this wasn't a time to be lazy
But time to drive those ghosts crazy!

All the disembodied ghouls
Were filling up the glass beakers
As the cats were corralling them
Using their musical loudspeakers!

With a little bit of dance
And a little bit of club,
With a little bit of trance
And by a little bit of dub.

Never giving anything ghostly
Even any single chance,
And with a bit of perfect timing
Using their evil catty glance...

Meowing while they were mixing,
Attacking in record scratches,
They were cleaning out that house!
Catching those ghosts in big batches!

It was quite a ghost-busting scene,
And it all happened on Halloween.
Soon, no more ghosts would be seen,
And that place would be totally clean....

And what more could I say about those cats and all that?
I'm afraid that's all that I could ever really say about that...

Moments we'll never forget

Fun with words

The tranquility of synchronicity is serendipity

Creativity runs in circles

"Some sketchy stuff"

"Unmetered and unhinged"

Road-Racer

I put my sunglasses on as I turned the key.
Opening the hood
With the catches unclasped,
My engine's understood
And its power is grasped.

This race through life can't be lost,
Despite the trouble or increasing cost.
The finish line must come before my fall
With a finely tuned motor that will never stall.

Starting it up at the top dead-center
As the flywheel spun up very fast.
Then new dynamics would quickly enter,
A balanced harmonic to always last.

And as the crankshaft spun, so did I.
Reaching out, I would touch the sky.
Then my mind began its new dreaming
As all the headers fired into screaming.

Revving my engine as it comes awake,
Revolutions unbound by the noise it will make.
As the cylinders cycled, the transmission transformed,
The suspension stabilized as new roads were formed.

Speeding down the shorter highways of life,
The blinkers blurred as I passed them by.
Like driving on the edge of a razor-sharp knife,
Before the roads of life would say goodbye.

Like poetry in motion as I shifted the gears,
The fire of devotion burned through my fears.
With messages of light and true emotion,
The road signs flashed by as if in slow motion.

Pressing the red button!
Kicked my turbocharger on,
Racing words against time
Before my daylight is gone.

Running the stop lights,
All bridges will be crossed,
And my engine will rage on
Before its meaning is lost.

And I was contemplating
As the camshafts were rotating,
Laughing at the constrictions
And overcoming the frictions.

Mastering the turns without any fear
As my overdrive gear drew ever near,
And double-checking my gauges,
Running this race of life through the ages.

In this dashboard, I was carefully learning,
Gaining the subtlety of a clear discerning,
With mag wheels intentionally burning.
As my mind was quickly shifting and turning.

The coil packs sparked a brighter blue,
Increasing their currents in a clearer hue.
With a windshield clean and glass unbroken,
Now knowing what words should be spoken.

With leather gloves on the steering wheel,
Controlling my engine's fiery steel.
Let the checkered flags all be damned—
I'll damn well do just as I've planned.

Revving the motor within my mind
Like the other race cars of my own kind.
In lanes, no center line will ever divide,
Racing by our words both far and wide.

Loosening life as lubrication demands,
Synchronizing gears by our commands.
Surpassing all the Sunday drivers,
I'll take my place with the road race survivors.

Clowning Around

One night I was just trying to take a walk downtown,
Then surprise, surprise... I ran into a creepy clown.
He started running down the street, coming straight at me!
But I quickly jumped to the side behind the nearest tree...
In no uncertain terms, I told him...

"Listen, buddy, leave me alone. take a hike!
I never associate with clowns who don't ride a bike.
Better yet, all my clown friends have at least one monkey, too.
You have neither. what the hell is wrong with you..."

"You run at me as if you want to engage in some sort of struggle.
You aren't even a respectable clown though....
You don't even have any colored balls to juggle!"

But he responded....

"You will be very sorry because I do have a large knife...
I'll filet your innards and then I will take your pathetic life!"

But then I let him know...

"I'm sorry, Bozo, but tonight's advantage is clearly with me."
I then pulled out my little Ruger .380 LCP.
It may be small, but it kicks like a big horse,
And it will fill any creepy clown with some bloody remorse.

In the future, to be safe and ensure that I stay alive,
I'll use my .380 as a backup, and pack a .45...

Santa's Workshop

Through a very strange twist of my daily fate,
I would be celebrating Christmas just a little bit late,
Because I was taken away in the middle of the night
And the escorts who took me were an unexpected sight.

There were three elves that arrived on a rocket sled.
They promptly threw me on board and in unison said,
"We hear you're a jack of all trades and master of a few.
"There are problems that need fixing; we've so much to do."

They reminded me of the munchkins in The Wizard of Oz,
So, I entertained their mission for this unknown cause.
And away we all flew to the North Pole (or so they said),
And it was kind of fun flying on that little red rocket sled.

Landing at the "sledport" with twinkling lights all around,
I saw a large group of elves waiting for us on the ground.
Many other rocket sleds were coming to land, too,
Each with an unwitting passenger having something to do.

And then up comes a large man in a sparkling white suit,
Saying, "You help the elves while I plan my delivery route.
They're all old school and need to pull out of their funk.
Bring them up to date on all this modern-day junk.

"We were hoping that older gifts would come back in style,
But it doesn't look hopeful, and we've waited quite a while.
Kids want electronic things that light up, beep, and buzz,
And my elves don't know what any of that new stuff does.

"So, I need you recruits to help and do the best that you can.
Christmas is coming and we must deliver according to plan.
Help make all the children happy and so very much more!
You'll each be given gift certificates for your favorite store!"

And all of us vowed to help and do our very best.
We would show them how to pass this technological test,
Carefully instructing them throughout the night
About gadgets and gizmos and putting batteries in right.

I thought it was a little strange seeing Santa in sparkly white,
So, I asked, "Where's the old red outfit? You just don't look right."
He said, "I'm up to speed because Santa is always very astute.
I got a new rocket sled man! I needed a flame-retardant suit!"

Country Boy

I drive a jacked-up pickup truck,
And I got some toilet paper for my butt.
I gots the most darlin' country girl
Who can make a pot pie out of squirrel.

I got the smarts to stay alive.
This country boy's gonna survive.
I can grow me some new potatoes
In a garden I can make from a tire.

I can make catsup out of turmatos
And roast possum over an open fire.
I ain't worried about no virus,
Ain't listenen to any o that hype.

I got that weed on past the cornfield,
And I can make me a corn cob pipe.
I got those tractors I'm always drivin'.
This country boy's good at survivin'.

Got those cows I'm always a milkin',
A couple o' barns that's filled with hay.
And old Granny can do the quiltin'
And my cousin, the preacher, can pray.

I ain't like any of them pretty city folk.
I'm a man that's plain down-to-earth.
And my momma can switch you in a second,
So you'd best be given er a wide berth.

Got my shotgun and Pap's old pistol,
And my little 22 rifle and more
Can shoot any of the varmints up yonder
And shoot the locks off any barn door.

I can get honey from most any beehive.
This country boy's gonna stay alive…

Red Ferrari

The bulls were perplexed as they ran through the streets,
While all the screaming people ran away,
By the mother of all charges that a matador meets,
The bulls were determined to win it this day.

Those stupid little people would be bloody and red,
Dismembered by the horns of an angry herd,
Being trodden asunder and stomped on the head,
By the anger of the bulls that this rally had spurred.

But their Hawaiian shirts were all yellow and blue,
Those confusing clothes on the people who fled,
Some orange was there but of a lighter hue,
As the bulls were desperately seeking out red.

Pursuing the prize of a glimpse of red
A big one awaited just ahead in their path.
The bulls all agreed and enough was said–
It was the mother of all targets in a bull's bloodbath.

For every victory technology steals
Animals grunt as they lose their way,
Engines of steel with their rubber wheels
Would steal the battle from the bulls today.

Though the running bulls were very quick,
They couldn't keep up although they tried.
Not the best target that a bull could pick
And not one red Ferrari has ever died…

ACKNOWLEDGMENTS

And thank you if you've managed to read through all of this! I write these poems on a whim as I go about my days at work and driving. Sometimes on the back porch as well in the warmer months. And although I can't quite put my finger on it or explain it, I feel that there's something larger at play. I try to write these poems to apply them to many people in various circumstances. Perhaps even just a couple of words, a stanza, or even entire poems at times. I hope some of them do speak to you in some way. We live in such an ever-demanding and complex world. At times just waiting to strip your inner humanity from you if it can.

My own life hasn't worked out so perfectly either,
But has anyones? Really? I could certainly hope so, but that doesn't usually seem to be the case these days. And perhaps it never was. So often when I write these, I can feel some sort of great happiness or satisfaction that almost seems to come from outside of me. I can't explain it in any way that you would understand. But I can certainly feel it. The rush of emotions, and the release of expression. It's made me a little bit more human; I think. And I wouldn't trade the experience of all of it for anything. We have such a short time here. But I really feel that this is just a small part of the whole.

There's great power in your own spirit when you allow it to open up to become weak so that it might become strong. And I don't think that it ever really dies then…

Thank you to the fine editors and publications where these poems, sometimes in earlier versions, first appeared:

The Watershed Journal: "Such a Thing!," "Changes," "Firefly," "What's it worth?," "Preemptive Paranoia," "Playhouses," "Rubber Shoes," "Just Another Mother's Day," "Snowballs," "Funeral For a Son," "The Mothers of Our Past," "Atomic Swing," "Low-skilled," "Winter," "Pencils and Papers," "Dandelions," "Painted Grey," "Green," "Little Birdies," "Colors," "Let You Go," "Questions," "Supercharger," "Twirling," "Endless Summer," "Girl," "Robot Rules," "Christmas Kitten."

ABOUT THE AUTHOR

Kirke Wise is a lifelong resident of the North-western Pennsylvania wilds. He has had many varied interests and hobbies during this time. These include organic gardening, raising chickens, living off-grid, and creating renewable energy projects. He has spent the last thirty-five years of his work career in the high-technology sector as a field electronic service technician. Kirke has worked to install and maintain many public service and industry radio communications networks within that time. Kirke first got his start in electronics at a young age. He would tear apart electronics and repurpose the parts to build devices.

Later, he started as a consultant building, designing, and programming several state-of-the-art computer-controlled industrial monitoring and control systems before delving into two-way radio communications. Today, his more recent hobby is writing poetry. He treats writing much like designing and building devices. Kirke has been published a few times in newsprint and in a couple of poetry collections. Kirke has recently expanded his talents to write custom poems for authors to include in their nonfiction and fiction works.

Kirke Wise is one of the four founders of The Watershed Journal. They have published quarterly magazines since 2018. Kirke's work has been published in each of the twenty-two issues thus far. Kirke presently serves as President of The Board of Directors for The Watershed Journal Literary Group, the umbrella organization that covers the magazine and the Watershed Books bookstore. You can learn more about Kirke at www.kirkewise.com

www.ingramcontent.com/pod-product-compliance
Lightning Source LLC
Chambersburg PA
CBHW011227120626
46549CB00008B/3180